THE CHILDREN'S FIRST ATLAS

Text by Neil Morris

Illustrated by Illustratori Associati Boni-Galante

HORUS EDITIONS

Published by Horus Editions Limited,
52-56 Osnaburgh Street,
London NW1 3NS

British Library Cataloguing in Publication Data for this book are available from the British Library.

ISBN 1-899762-05-1 Printed in Belgium

Contents

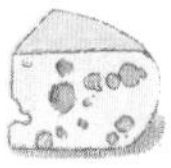

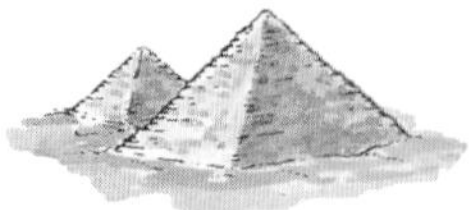

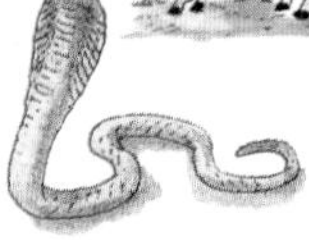

How to use this atlas

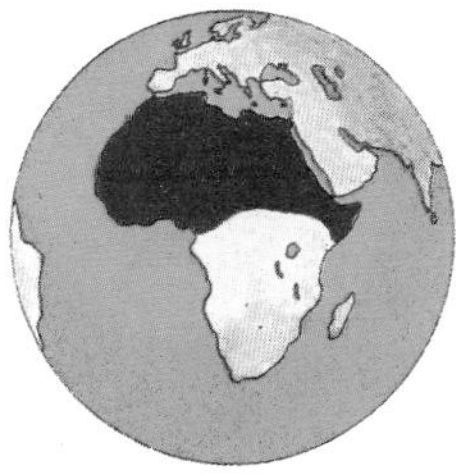

'he small globe in each ection shows in red where ıe countries are located.

ligh areas of ground are hown in two ways: the ighest mountains appear o be more pointed and re coloured white.

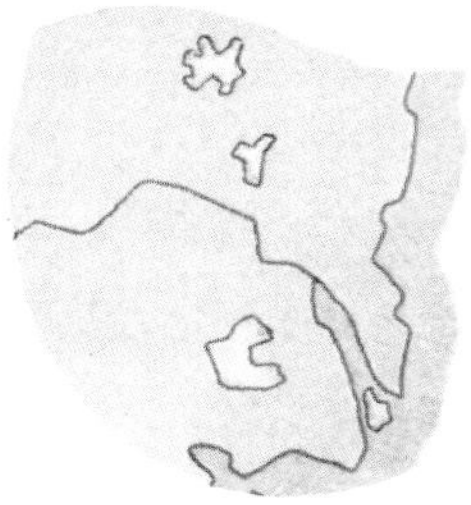

ieas and oceans are oloured blue. Small areas of blue on the land are akes. Rivers are shown as lue lines.

ome lakes shown do not ppear all year round but dry p during certain times of the ear. These are indicated by roken lines.

Geographical features of pecial interest are ometimes pinpointed by ymbols.

This atlas is a book of maps and information about the countries of the world. Each section has a map of an area of the world, accompanied by an introductory text and information about points of interest.

The maps show geographical features, such as mountains, rivers and lakes, that are important to a particular area of the world. Capitals are shown for most countries, as well as other noteworthy cities.

Symbols represent areas where, for example, fruits and vegetables might grow or where industries, such as mining or fishing, are located. The symbols also show where plants and animals live. Some symbols locate famous buildings, and others picture people who live in a region.

Red lines mark each country's borders. State borders are shown in green.

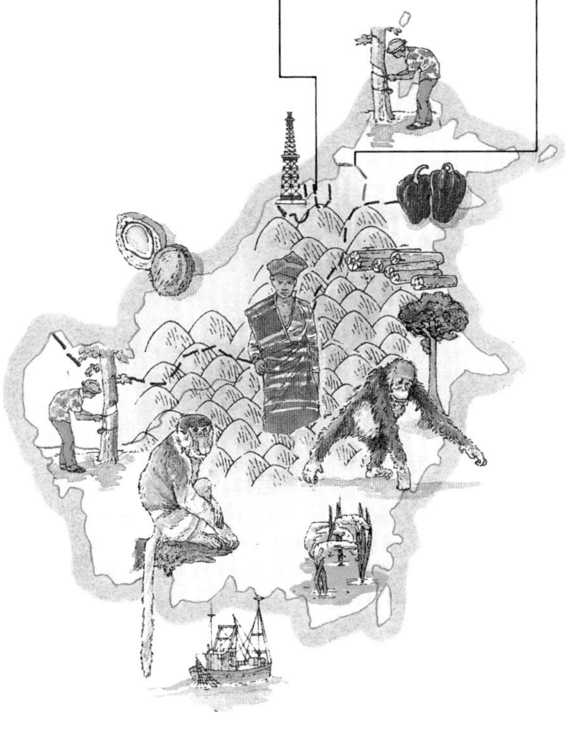

Other symbols on the maps may show produce, industry, natural resources, animals, people, vegetation or mountains.

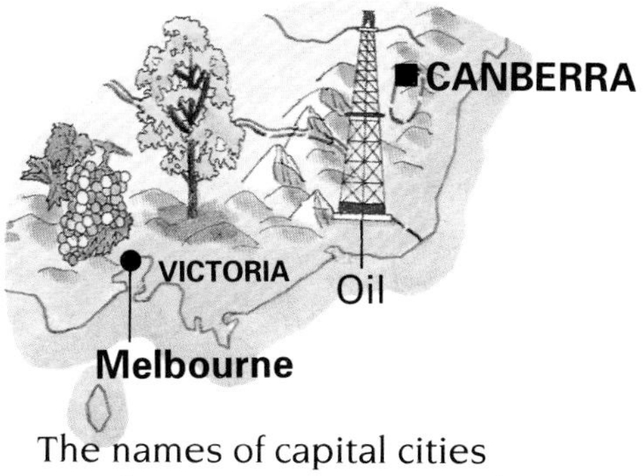
CANBERRA
VICTORIA
Oil
Melbourne

The names of capital cities are always written in capital letters and sometimes marked by a square on the map. Other cities are shown by a dot.

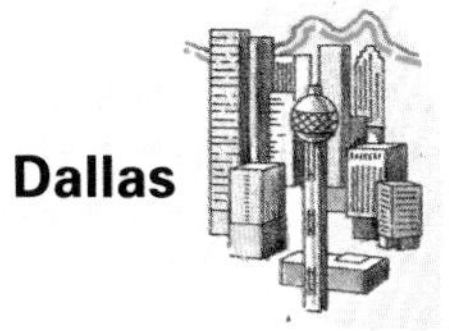
Dallas

Certain cities have interesting buildings, and in some cases pictures of these buildings mark the city, as well as a square or a dot.

Trees of different types show the various types of vegetation around the world.

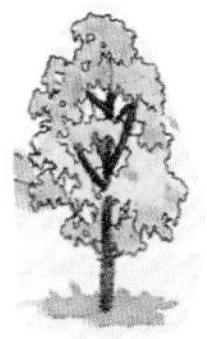

Broad-leaved trees grow where the weather is warmer.

Spruce and fir trees grow in cold areas.

Rainforest trees show hot, wet, tropical areas.

The scale lets you estimate the size of each country and how far one place is from another. Each map is drawn to a different scale.

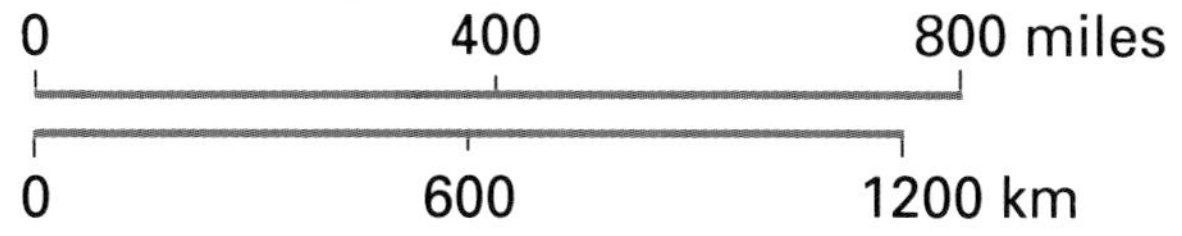
0
400
800 miles
0
600
1200 km

The World

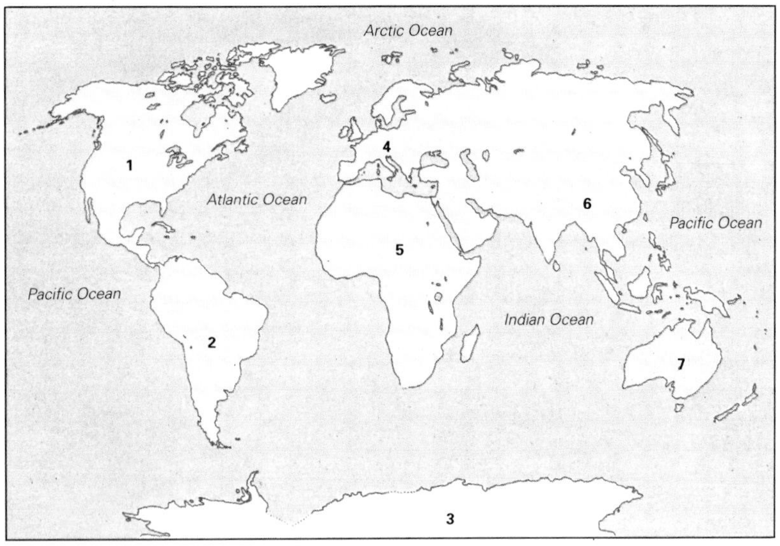
Arctic Ocean
Atlantic Ocean
Pacific Ocean
Pacific Ocean
Indian Ocean
1
2
3
4
5
6
7

If the surface of the round Earth were stretched out, it would make a flat map of the world, with the Pacific Ocean split in two.

From outer space, the Earth looks blue, since so much of its surface is covered by water. There are 4 major bodies of water – the Pacific, Atlantic, Indian and Arctic oceans.

The oceans are separated by large areas of land. These are the Earth's 7 continents. The continents of Asia, Africa and Europe form more than half the Earth's total landmass. North and South America make up a long stretch of land between the Pacific and Atlantic oceans. Antarctica lies around the South Pole. Australia is the smallest continent.

Throughout the world, weather conditions – or climate – are very different. A region's climate is affected by its location, by how high it is above sea level, by how close it is to mountains or oceans, and by local winds.

The Arctic (North Pole) and Antarctic regions are freezing cold. Below the Arctic are frozen

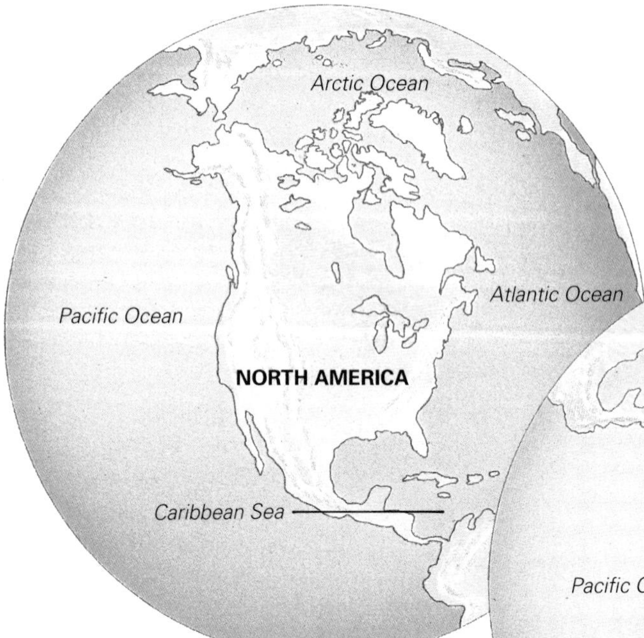
Arctic Ocean
Pacific Ocean
Atlantic Ocean
NORTH AMERICA
Caribbean Sea

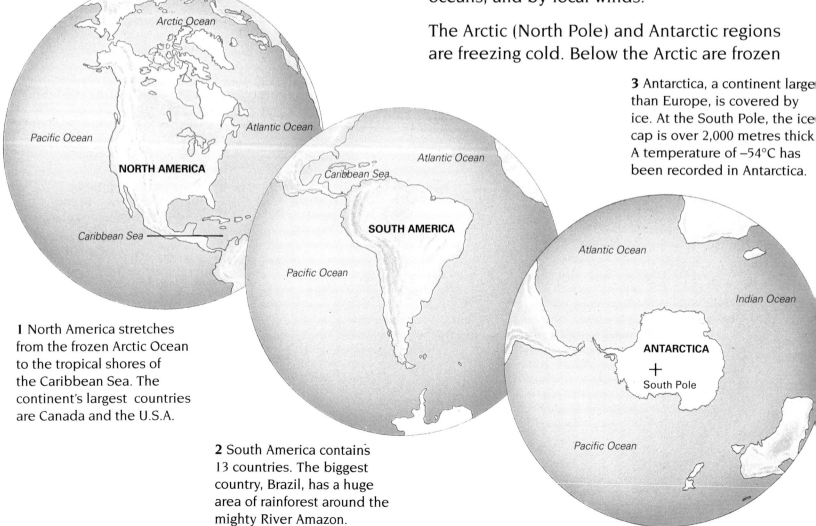

1 North America stretches from the frozen Arctic Ocean to the tropical shores of the Caribbean Sea. The continent's largest countries are Canada and the U.S.A.

Atlantic Ocean
Caribbean Sea
SOUTH AMERICA
Pacific Ocean

2 South America contains 13 countries. The biggest country, Brazil, has a huge area of rainforest around the mighty River Amazon.

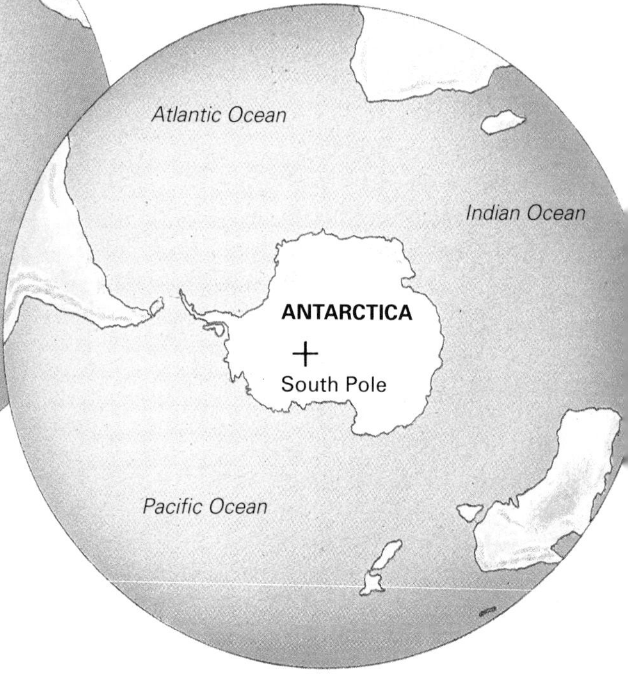
Atlantic Ocean
Indian Ocean
ANTARCTICA
South Pole
Pacific Ocean

3 Antarctica, a continent larger than Europe, is covered by ice. At the South Pole, the ice cap is over 2,000 metres thick. A temperature of –54°C has been recorded in Antarctica.

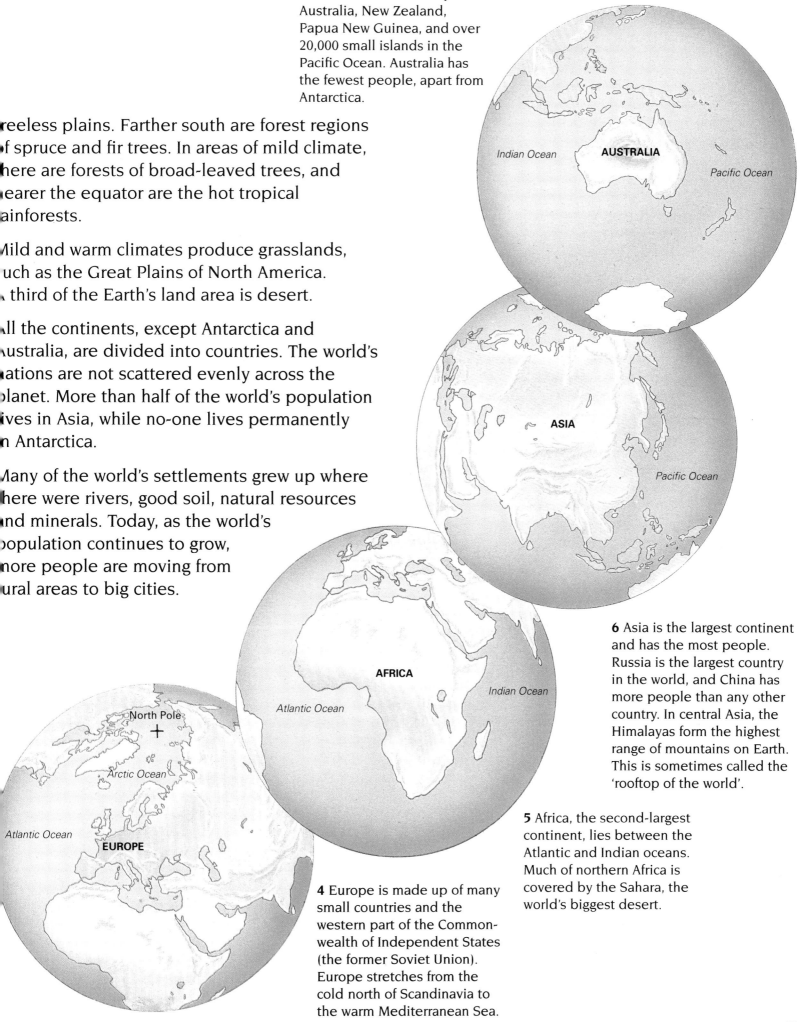

7 Australasia is made up of Australia, New Zealand, Papua New Guinea, and over 20,000 small islands in the Pacific Ocean. Australia has the fewest people, apart from Antarctica.

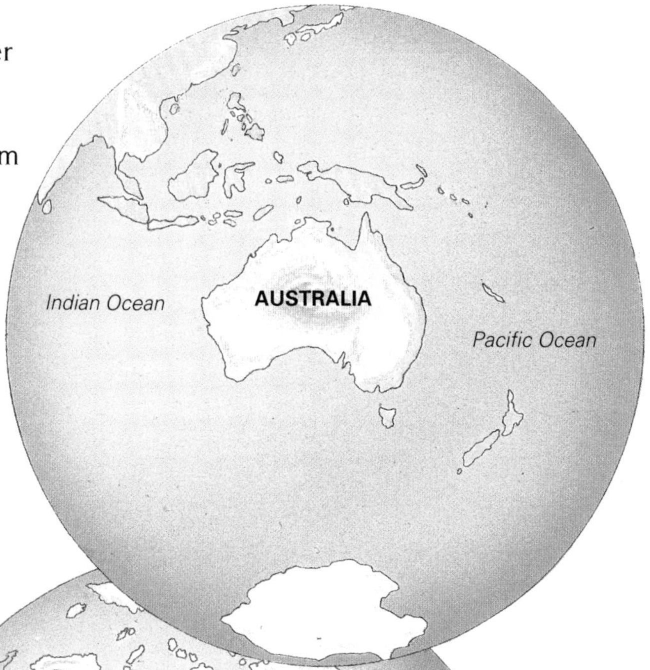
AUSTRALIA
Indian Ocean
Pacific Ocean

reeless plains. Farther south are forest regions f spruce and fir trees. In areas of mild climate, here are forests of broad-leaved trees, and earer the equator are the hot tropical ainforests.

Aild and warm climates produce grasslands, uch as the Great Plains of North America. third of the Earth's land area is desert.

ll the continents, except Antarctica and ustralia, are divided into countries. The world's ations are not scattered evenly across the lanet. More than half of the world's population ives in Asia, while no-one lives permanently n Antarctica.

Aany of the world's settlements grew up where here were rivers, good soil, natural resources nd minerals. Today, as the world's opulation continues to grow, nore people are moving from ural areas to big cities.

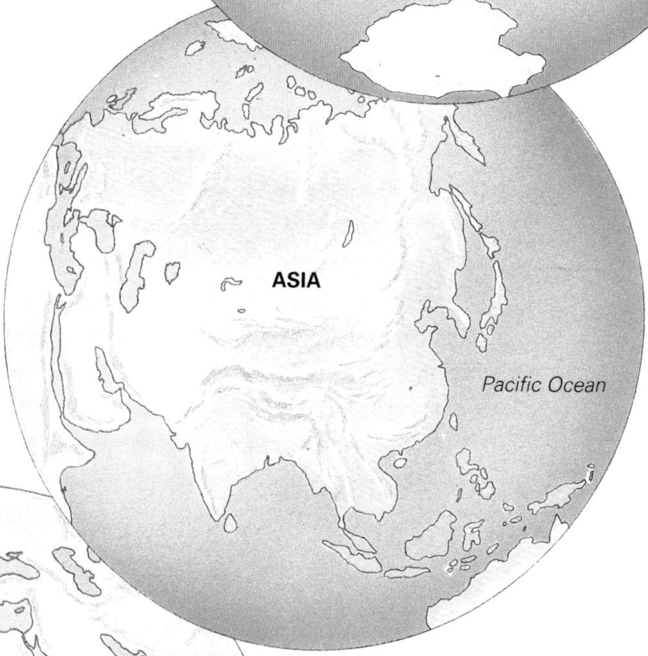
ASIA
Pacific Ocean

6 Asia is the largest continent and has the most people. Russia is the largest country in the world, and China has more people than any other country. In central Asia, the Himalayas form the highest range of mountains on Earth. This is sometimes called the 'rooftop of the world'.

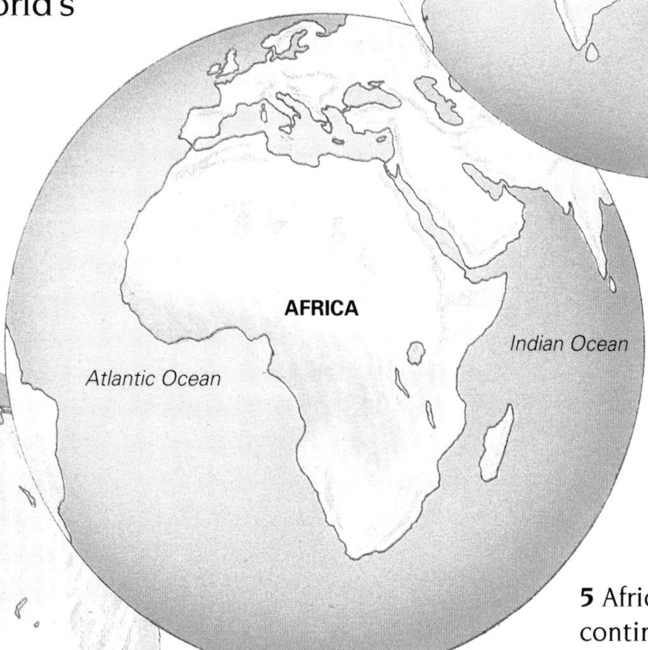
AFRICA
Atlantic Ocean
Indian Ocean

5 Africa, the second-largest continent, lies between the Atlantic and Indian oceans. Much of northern Africa is covered by the Sahara, the world's biggest desert.

North Pole
Arctic Ocean
Atlantic Ocean
EUROPE

4 Europe is made up of many small countries and the western part of the Commonwealth of Independent States (the former Soviet Union). Europe stretches from the cold north of Scandinavia to the warm Mediterranean Sea.

North Europe

The British Isles consists of the large islands of Great Britain (England, Scotland, Wales) and Ireland, plus many smaller islands. The United Kingdom is a country made up of Great Britain and Northern Ireland. The southern part of Ireland (the Republic of Ireland) is an independent country. Cows and sheep graze on pastures all over the British Isles. Oil and gas are found in the North Sea off Scotland.

Norway, Sweden, Denmark, Finland and Iceland make up Scandinavia. Huge forests in Scandinavia provide wood to make paper and furniture. These countries also have large fishing fleets.

Greenland, a part of Denmark, is a very large island. Most of it lies within the Arctic Circle. Few people live there.

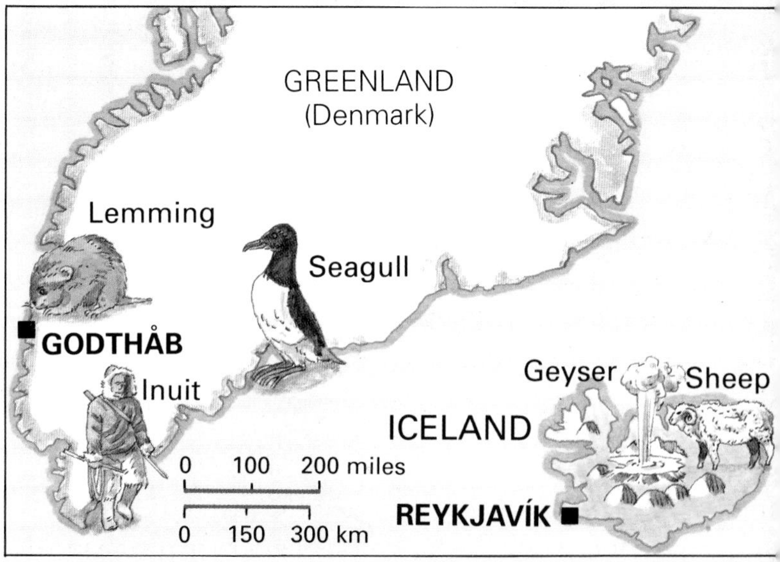

GREENLAND
(Denmark)
Lemming
Seagull
GODTHÅB
Inuit
Geyser
Sheep
ICELAND
0 100 200 miles
0 150 300 km
REYKJAVÍK

More About . . .

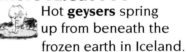

Hot **geysers** spring up from beneath the frozen earth in Iceland.

Big Ben is a 13.8 tonne bell in the clock tower of Westminster, London.

Tweed is a thick wool cloth from Scotland, used to make clothes.

Hadrian's Wall was built by the ancient Romans for protectio

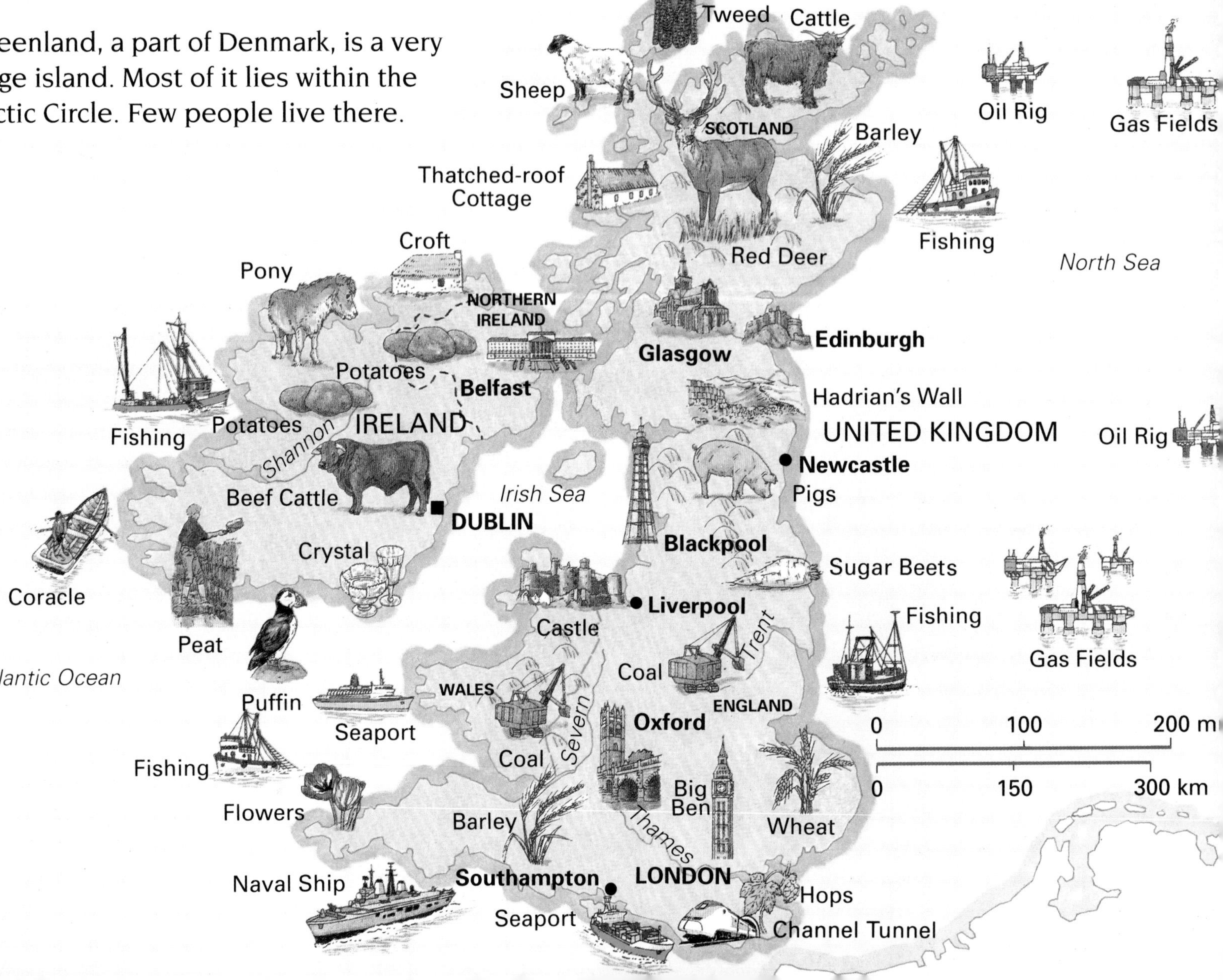

Tweed
Cattle
Sheep
Oil Rig
Gas Fields
SCOTLAND
Barley
Thatched-roof Cottage
Fishing
Croft
Red Deer
North Sea
Pony
NORTHERN IRELAND
Edinburgh
Glasgow
Potatoes
Belfast
Hadrian's Wall
Fishing
Potatoes
IRELAND
UNITED KINGDOM
Oil Rig
Shannon
Newcastle
Beef Cattle
Irish Sea
Pigs
DUBLIN
Blackpool
Crystal
Sugar Beets
Coracle
Liverpool
Fishing
Peat
Castle
Trent
Gas Fields
Atlantic Ocean
Coal
WALES
ENGLAND
Puffin
Oxford
Seaport
Severn
0 100 200 m
Coal
0 150 300 km
Fishing
Big Ben
Flowers
Barley
Thames
Wheat
Naval Ship
Southampton
LONDON
Hops
Seaport
Channel Tunnel

)id You Know?

'here are about 60,000 lakes n Finland.

\t Legoland in the Danish own of Billund, 38 million .ego bricks are used o make model tatues, buildings ınd animals.

Norway is more than twice ıs large as England, but England has over 0 times as many ɔeople.

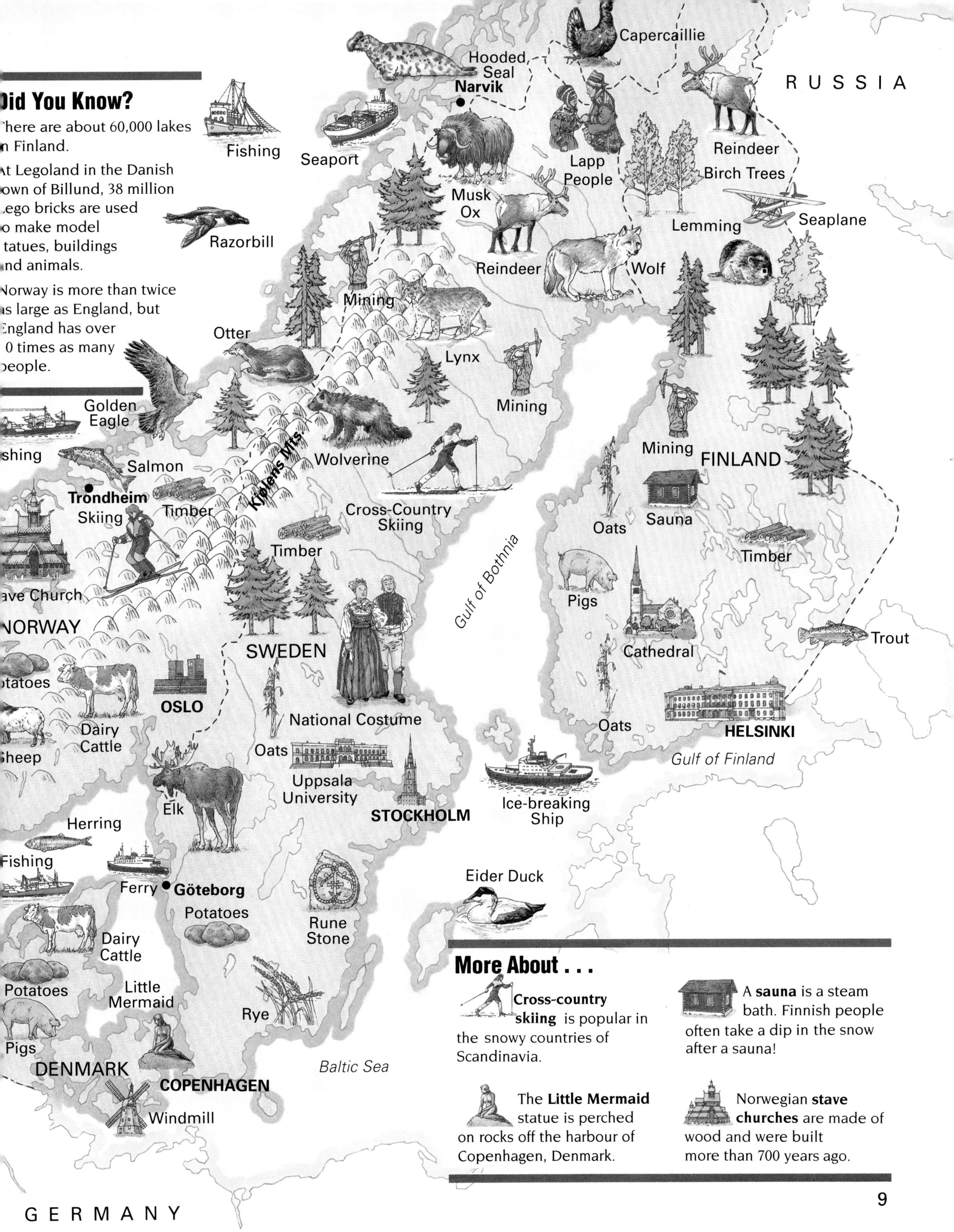

Capercaillie
Hooded Seal
Narvik
RUSSIA
Fishing
Seaport
Lapp People
Reindeer
Birch Trees
Musk Ox
Seaplane
Lemming
Razorbill
Reindeer
Wolf
Mining
Otter
Lynx
Mining
Golden Eagle
shing
Salmon
Wolverine
Mining
FINLAND
Trondheim
Skiing
Timber
Kjølens Mts.
Cross-Country Skiing
Oats
Sauna
Timber
Timber
Gulf of Bothnia
ave Church
Pigs
NORWAY
SWEDEN
Cathedral
Trout
otatoes
OSLO
Dairy Cattle
National Costume
Oats
HELSINKI
heep
Oats
Gulf of Finland
Uppsala University
Elk
STOCKHOLM
Ice-breaking Ship
Herring
Fishing
Ferry
Göteborg
Eider Duck
Potatoes
Rune Stone
Dairy Cattle
Potatoes
Little Mermaid
Rye
Pigs
DENMARK
COPENHAGEN
Baltic Sea
Windmill
GERMANY

More About . . .

Cross-country skiing is popular in the snowy countries of Scandinavia.

The **Little Mermaid** statue is perched on rocks off the harbour of Copenhagen, Denmark.

A **sauna** is a steam bath. Finnish people often take a dip in the snow after a sauna!

Norwegian **stave churches** are made of wood and were built more than 700 years ago.

France and the Low Countries

France is the largest country in western Europe. It has rich farmlands, and its mild climate is ideal for growing wheat, maize and barley. Grapes also grow here, and French wine is the most famous in the world. France is also well known for its fine food, in restaurants and in the home.

There are many beautiful French cities. Paris, the capital, is an important centre of art and learning. The main industrial region lies north of Paris. The Alps, in the south of France, are popular for skiing. The Riviera, along the Mediterranean coast, is a region with many beach resorts.

The Low Countries consist of Belgium, the Netherlands (Holland) and Luxembourg. Much of the Netherlands is below sea level. However, the Dutch people have built special dams called dikes to hold back the sea.

More About . . .

Truffles are mushroom-like plants that grow underground and have a special taste. Pigs and dogs are used for truffle hunting.

In the Netherlands, **windmills** are no longer used to pump floodwater from the land. Dikes have been built to keep the land dry.

The **Tour de France** is the best-known bicycle race in the world. Cyclists from many countries compete in it. The route covers 3,540 kilometres and ends in Paris.

TGV high-speed trains run from Paris to other French cities. They are the fastest passenger trains in the world.

Basque shepherds live in the foothills of the Pyrenees. The Basques speak their own language. Some Basques want their own state.

The **cave paintings** at Lascaux may be 17,000 years old. They show horses, deer and other animals. Tourists flock to Lascaux.

Did You Know?

Luxembourg has more than 100 castles, and many are partly in ruins. It has been called the 'Land of Haunted Castles'.

France, Belgium, the Netherlands and Luxembourg are all in the European Union. Its headquarters are in Brussels, Belgium's capital. The Union brings member countries closer together and helps them do business with each other. Other members are Denmark, Germany, Greece, Ireland, Italy, Portugal, Spain and the U.K.

Belgium has two groups of native people. Flemings speak Flemish, a form of Dutch, and Walloons speak a French dialect.

The city of Amsterdam, in the Netherlands, is built on about 100 islands, which are joined by a series of canals. At least 50 cars a year fall into the canals. There are special police to recover sunken cars and bikes.

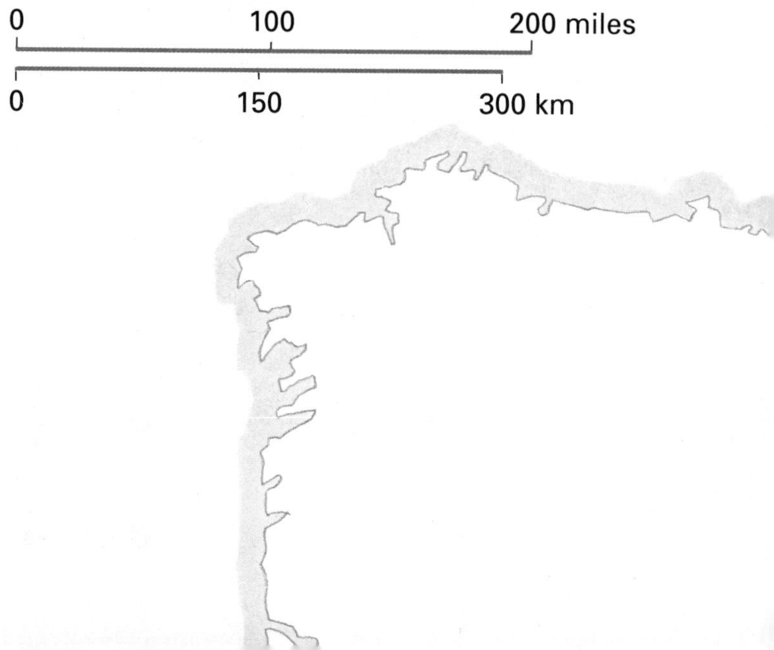
0
100
200 miles
0
150
300 km

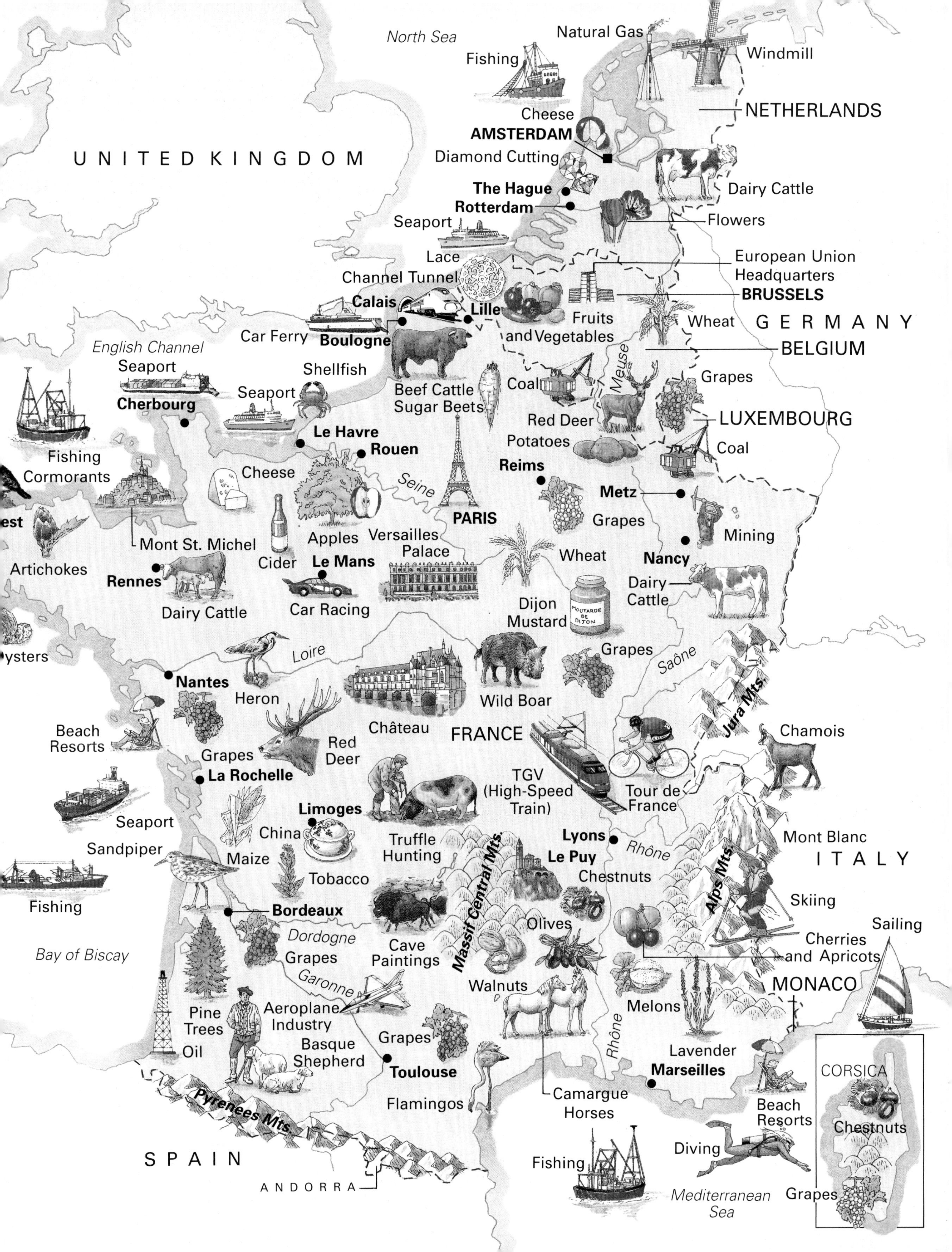
North Sea
Natural Gas
Fishing
Windmill
Cheese
AMSTERDAM
NETHERLANDS
UNITED KINGDOM
Diamond Cutting
The Hague
Rotterdam
Dairy Cattle
Seaport
Flowers
Lace
European Union
Headquarters
Channel Tunnel
BRUSSELS
Calais
Lille
Fruits
and Vegetables
Wheat
GERMANY
Car Ferry
Boulogne
BELGIUM
English Channel
Seaport
Shellfish
Grapes
Coal
Meuse
Seaport
Beef Cattle
Sugar Beets
Cherbourg
Red Deer
LUXEMBOURG
Le Havre
Potatoes
Coal
Fishing
Rouen
Cormorants
Cheese
Reims
Seine
Metz
est
Grapes
PARIS
Mining
Apples
Versailles
Palace
Mont St. Michel
Wheat
Artichokes
Cider
Le Mans
Nancy
Rennes
Dairy
Cattle
Dijon
Dairy Cattle
Car Racing
Mustard
MOUTARDE DE DIJON
Grapes
Loire
Saône
ysters
Nantes
Heron
Wild Boar
Jura Mts.
Beach
Resorts
Château
FRANCE
Chamois
Red
Deer
Grapes
La Rochelle
TGV
(High-Speed
Train)
Tour de
France
Limoges
Seaport
China
Truffle
Hunting
Lyons
Rhône
Mont Blanc
Sandpiper
Le Puy
ITALY
Maize
Massif Central Mts.
Chestnuts
Alps Mts.
Tobacco
Skiing
Fishing
Bordeaux
Sailing
Olives
Cherries
and Apricots
Dordogne
Cave
Paintings
Bay of Biscay
Grapes
MONACO
Garonne
Walnuts
Melons
Aeroplane
Industry
Pine
Trees
Grapes
Rhône
Basque
Shepherd
Lavender
Oil
Toulouse
Marseilles
CORSICA
Pyrenees Mts.
Camargue
Horses
Flamingos
Beach
Resorts
Chestnuts
SPAIN
Diving
Fishing
ANDORRA
Mediterranean
Sea
Grapes

Central Europe

Central Europe is dominated by Germany, a leading industrial nation. The Ruhr valley is a region of heavy industry, and the Rhine River is an important route for transporting cargo. Northern Germany has plains with fertile farmlands. Southern Germany has mountains and forests. Farther south are the countries of Switzerland and Austria. They are dominated by the mountains of the Alps.

To the east lie the Czech Republic, Slovakia and Poland. They are rich in natural resources and have large industries. Poland has steel and shipbuilding centres on the Baltic Sea. Farming is also important in these countries.

Fishing
Seaport
Seaport
Pigs
Lübeck
Hamburg
Elbe
Oil
Natural Gas
Sheep
Apples
Mining
Sugar Beets
Hannover
Barley
Coal
Rhine
Cologne Cathedral
Racing Pigeon
Cologne
Bonn
Mining
Half-timbered Houses
Beer
Wine
Frankfurt
Grapes
Trier
Castle
GERMANY
Grapes
Nuremberg
Market
FRANCE
Stuttgart
Buzzard
Black Forest
Hops
Neuschwanstein Castle
Watches
Zurich
Bodensee
Cheese
Chocolate
BERN
Innsbruck
SWITZERLAND
Dairy Cattle
Alps Mts.
Skiing
Red Cross
Lake Geneva
Matterhorn
ITALY

More About . . .

Neuschwanstein castle in Bavaria was built over 100 years ago for King Ludwig II.

Switzerland is famous for its watchmaking. Swiss **watches** and clocks are popular all over the world.

Bohemia is a region of the Czech Republic that is popular with tourists. **Bohemian glassware** is made there.

The **chamois** is a wild antelope the size of a goat. It lives in the mountains and eats herbs, flowers and pine shoots.

Bison were once found throughout Europe. Now only a few are left. Most live in a protected forest in Poland.

Lipizzaner horses are trained at the Spanish Riding School in Vienna, Austria. They put on impressive shows at home and abroad.

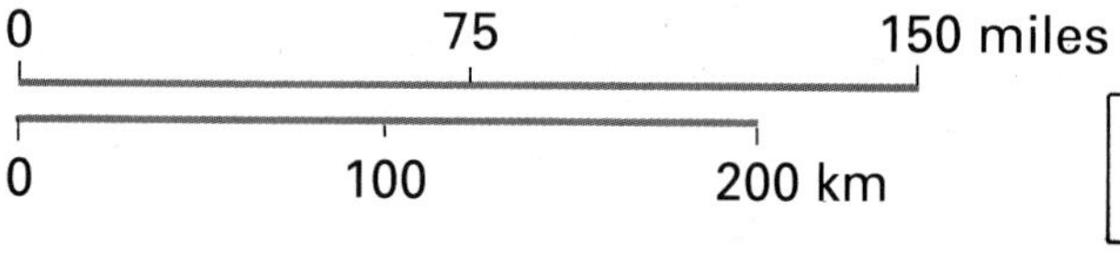

0
75
150 miles
0
100
200 km

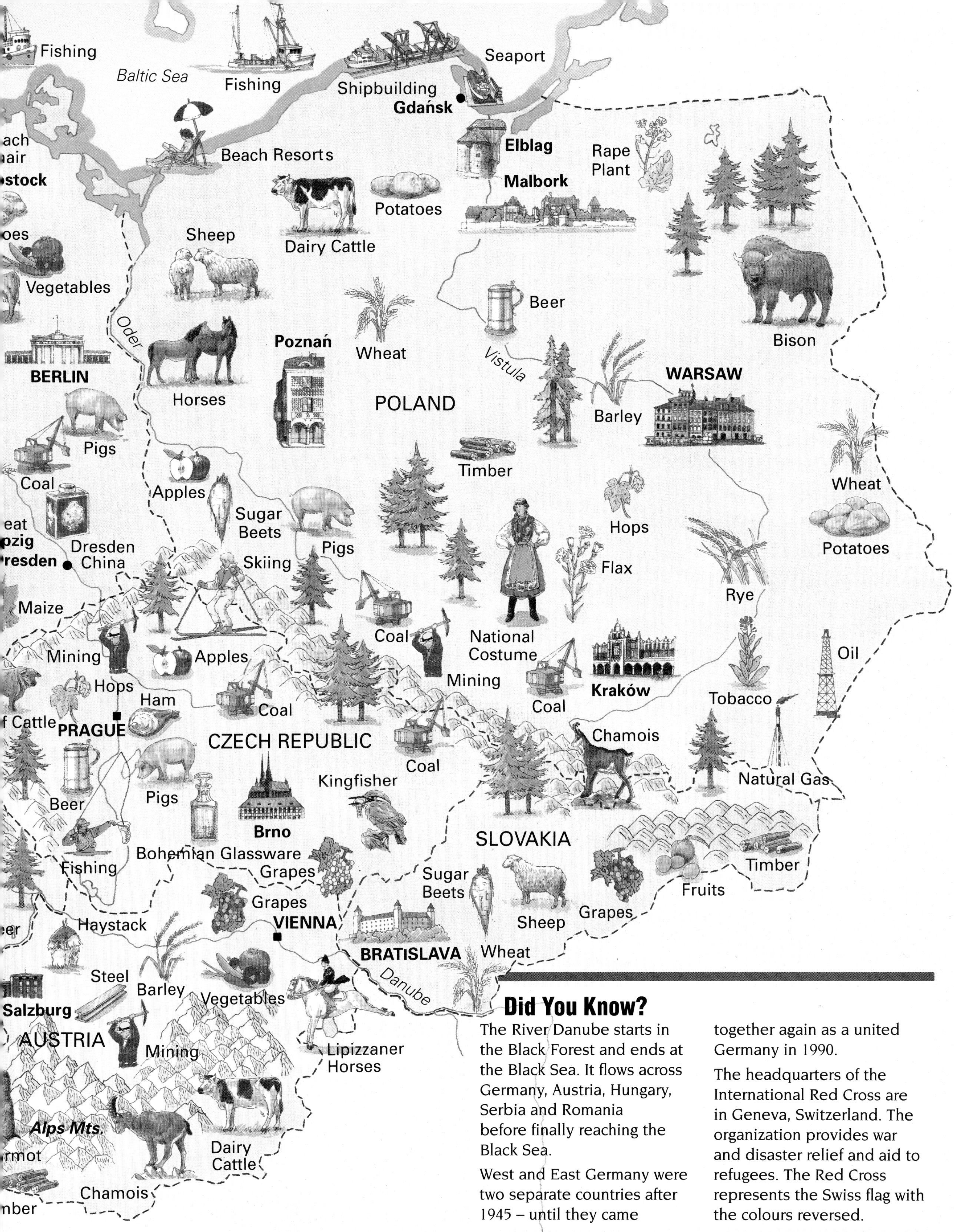

Fishing
Baltic Sea
Fishing
Shipbuilding
Seaport
Gdańsk
Beach Resorts
Elblag
Malbork
Rape Plant
Potatoes
Sheep
Dairy Cattle
Vegetables
Beer
Oder
Poznań
Wheat
Vistula
Bison
BERLIN
Horses
POLAND
WARSAW
Barley
Pigs
Timber
Wheat
Coal
Apples
Sugar Beets
Hops
Potatoes
Dresden China
Pigs
Skiing
Flax
Rye
Maize
Coal
National Costume
Oil
Mining
Apples
Mining
Hops
Ham
Coal
Kraków
Tobacco
Coal
PRAGUE
Chamois
CZECH REPUBLIC
Coal
Natural Gas
Kingfisher
Beer
Pigs
Brno
SLOVAKIA
Timber
Bohemian Glassware
Fishing
Grapes
Sugar Beets
Fruits
Grapes
Sheep
Grapes
VIENNA
Haystack
BRATISLAVA
Wheat
Steel
Danube
Barley
Vegetables
Salzburg
AUSTRIA
Mining
Lipizzaner Horses
Alps Mts.
Dairy Cattle
Chamois

Did You Know?

The River Danube starts in the Black Forest and ends at the Black Sea. It flows across Germany, Austria, Hungary, Serbia and Romania before finally reaching the Black Sea.

West and East Germany were two separate countries after 1945 – until they came together again as a united Germany in 1990.

The headquarters of the International Red Cross are in Geneva, Switzerland. The organization provides war and disaster relief and aid to refugees. The Red Cross represents the Swiss flag with the colours reversed.

Spain, Portugal and Italy

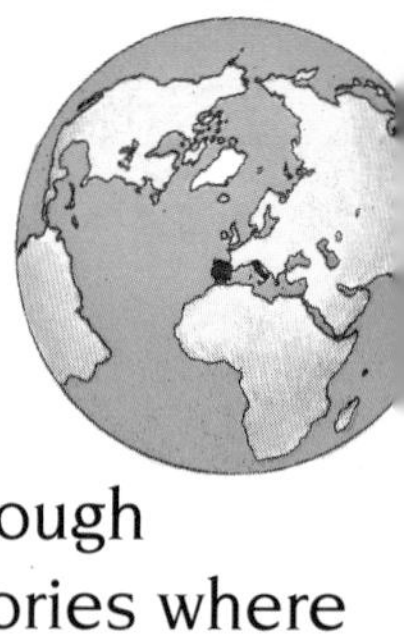

Several mountain ranges cross Spain. The highest mountains are the Pyrenees, between Spain and France, and the Sierra Nevada in the south. Many Spaniards now live and work in the towns, but others still work on the land, growing olives, citrus fruits and grapes. Portugal, to the west of Spain, is a much smaller country. Many Portuguese are fishermen or farmers.

Italy is a long, narrow country, with the Apennine Mountains running through its centre. In the north there are factories where cars and textiles are made. In the south farmers grow fruits, such as olives and oranges.

The climate in Spain, Portugal and Italy is mild. The region's beaches are popular holiday spots.

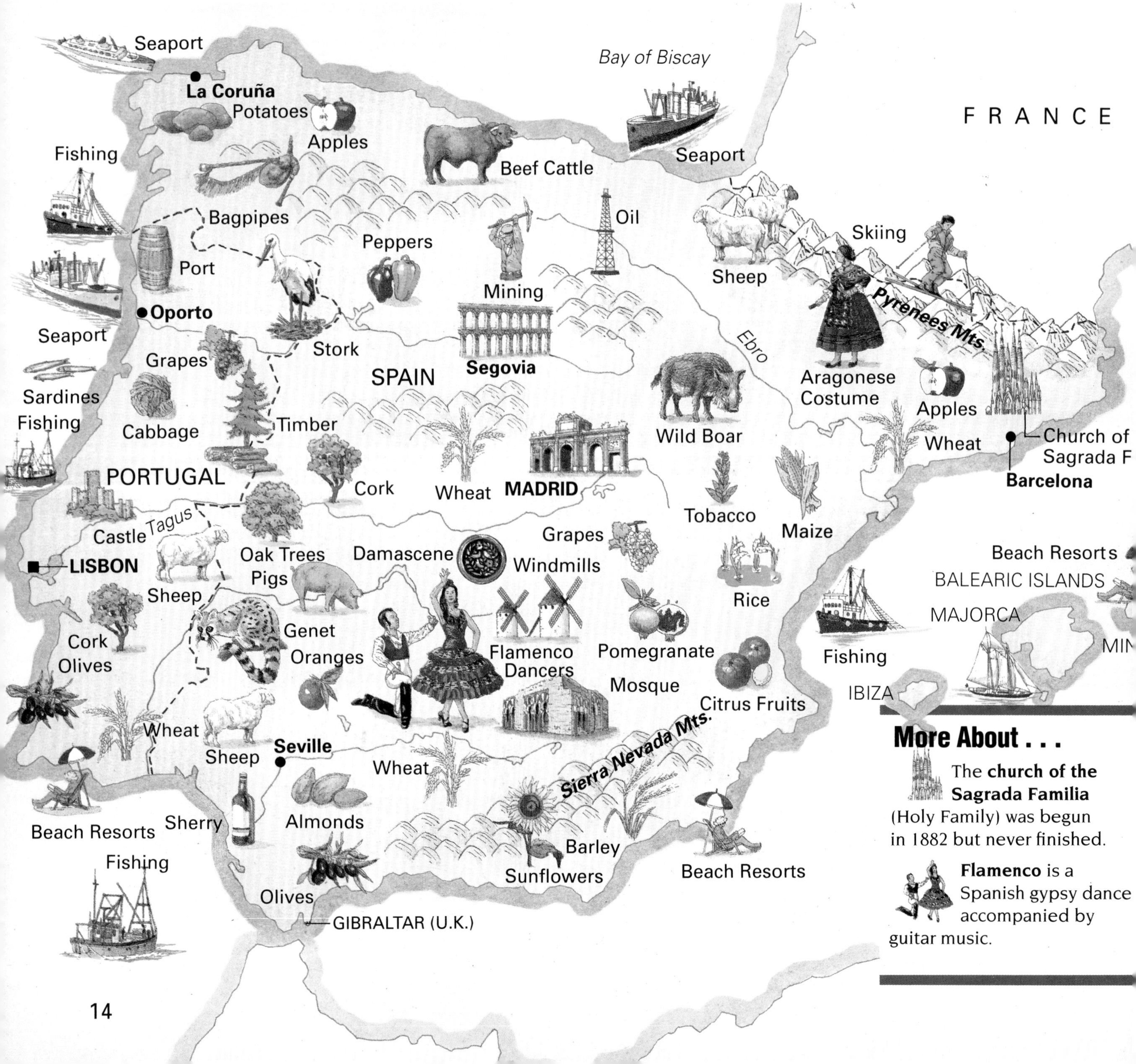

Seaport
La Coruña
Potatoes
Apples
Fishing
Bay of Biscay
Seaport
FRANCE
Beef Cattle
Bagpipes
Oil
Peppers
Port
Skiing
Sheep
Mining
Oporto
Pyrenees Mts.
Seaport
Stork
Ebro
Grapes
Segovia
SPAIN
Sardines
Aragonese Costume
Apples
Fishing
Cabbage
Timber
Wild Boar
Wheat
Church of Sagrada F
PORTUGAL
Cork
Wheat
MADRID
Barcelona
Tagus
Castle
Tobacco
Maize
Grapes
Oak Trees
Damascene
LISBON
Windmills
Beach Resorts
Pigs
BALEARIC ISLANDS
Sheep
Rice
MAJORCA
Genet
Cork
Flamenco Dancers
Pomegranate
Fishing
Olives
Oranges
MI
Mosque
Citrus Fruits
IBIZA
Wheat
Sierra Nevada Mts.
Sheep
Seville
Wheat
Beach Resorts
Sherry
Almonds
Barley
Sunflowers
Beach Resorts
Fishing
Olives
GIBRALTAR (U.K.)

More About . . .

The **church of the Sagrada Familia** (Holy Family) was begun in 1882 but never finished.

Flamenco is a Spanish gypsy dance accompanied by guitar music.

More About . . .

Cork is the bark of an oak tree used to make bottle stoppers.

People who visit Venice can travel along its canals in boats called **gondolas**.

In A.D. 79, Mount Vesuvius erupted. Volcanic ash buried the city of **Pompeii**.

Toledo, Spain, is famous for **damascene** – black metals inlaid with gold and silver thread.

Pasta is a popular food in Italy. It is traditionally made from wheat flour and water.

Saint Francis was born in **Assisi**, Italy. He gave up his wealth to live as a monk.

Did You Know?

The Vatican City is an independent state within the city of Rome. The Pope, head of the Roman Catholic Church, lives here. The Vatican City is also the smallest country in the world, with its own banking, telephone and postal systems.

On Sunday afternoons in Spain, large crowds gather to watch bullfights. The matador, in his sequined suit, flicks his bright-coloured cape at the charging bull and tries to avoid the bull's sharp horns.

Portugal is famous for port, a dark, strong red wine.

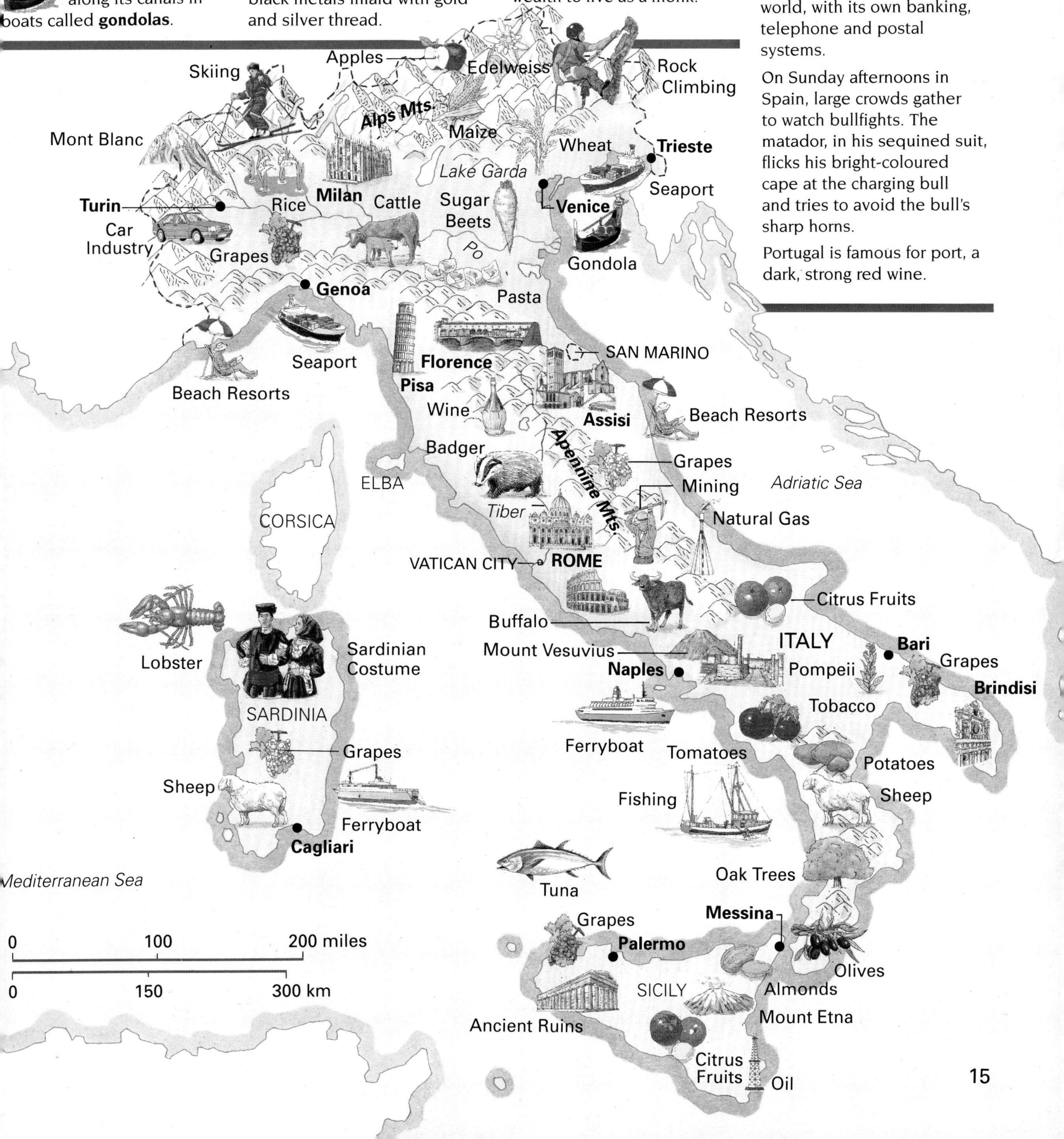

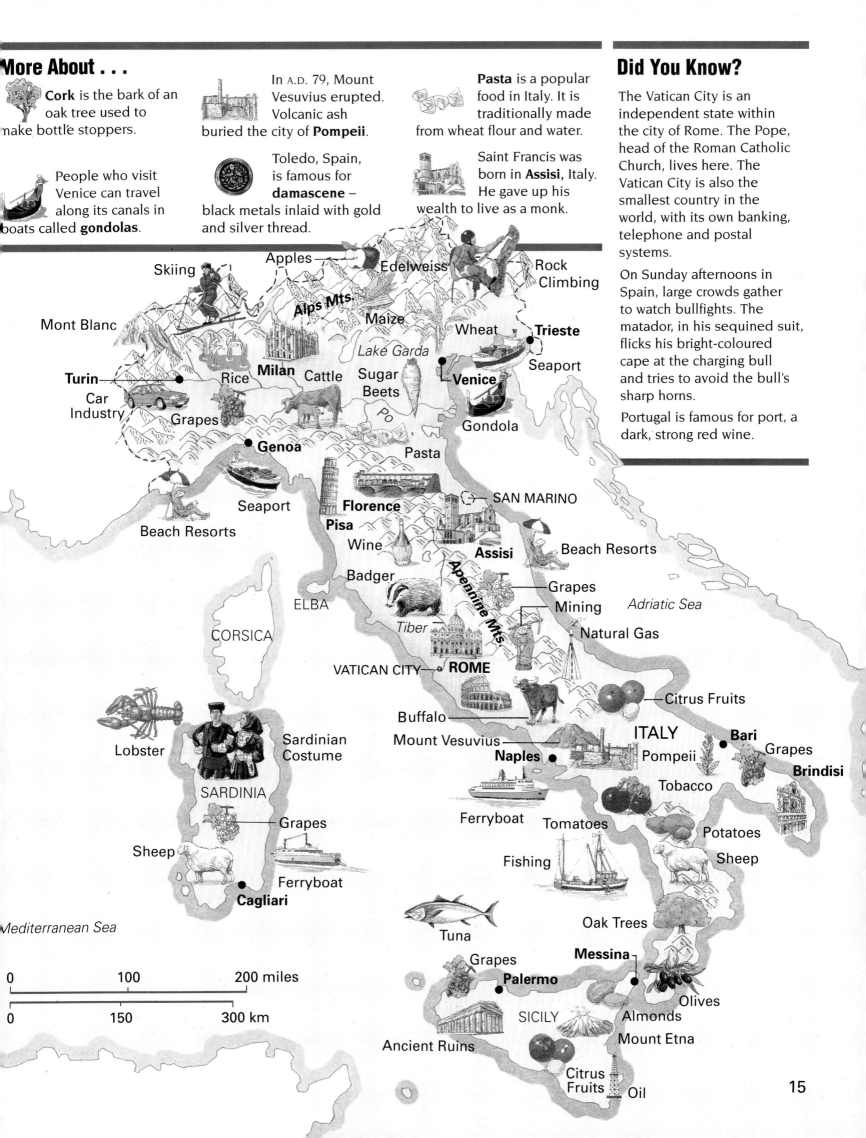

Skiing
Apples
Edelweiss
Rock Climbing
Alps Mts.
Maize
Mont Blanc
Wheat
Trieste
Lake Garda
Seaport
Turin
Rice
Milan
Cattle
Sugar Beets
Venice
Car Industry
Grapes
Po
Gondola
Genoa
Pasta
Seaport
Beach Resorts
Florence
Pisa
SAN MARINO
Wine
Assisi
Beach Resorts
Badger
Apennine Mts
Grapes
Mining
Adriatic Sea
ELBA
Tiber
Natural Gas
CORSICA
VATICAN CITY
ROME
Citrus Fruits
Buffalo
Lobster
Sardinian Costume
Mount Vesuvius
ITALY
Bari
Grapes
Naples
Pompeii
Brindisi
SARDINIA
Tobacco
Ferryboat
Tomatoes
Grapes
Potatoes
Sheep
Sheep
Fishing
Ferryboat
Cagliari
Mediterranean Sea
Oak Trees
Tuna
Grapes
Messina
Palermo
0
100
200 miles
0
150
300 km
Olives
SICILY
Almonds
Mount Etna
Ancient Ruins
Citrus Fruits
Oil

Southeast Europe

Hungary, Serbia, Croatia, Romania, Bulgaria and Greece are all part of southeast Europe. Budapest, the capital of Hungary, lies on the banks of the River Danube, which flows south into Serbia – one of the 6 separate republics that formerly made up the country of Yugoslavia. Differences between the 2 largest republics, Serbia and Croatia, led to civil war in 1991.

The Danube continues its journey to the Black Sea, forming the border between Romania and Bulgaria. Both countries have high mountain ranges: the Carpathians and the Transylvanian Alps in Romania; the Balkans in Bulgaria.

Albania is a small, poor country on the Adriatic Sea. To the south is the mainland of Greece, with its many islands. Tourism is very important to Greece. People come to visit the ancient ruins and to enjoy the country's islands and beaches.

Did You Know?

The ancient Olympic Games were first held at Olympia, Greece, in 776 B.C. The first modern Olympics were held in Athens in 1896.

Count Dracula, the infamous vampire, is supposed to have come from Transylvania, a region of Romania.

Skopje, the capital of the Yugoslav republic of Macedonia, has had a difficult history. In 1689 it was burned down to stop the spread of cholera disease, and in 1963 it was almost destroyed by an earthquake.

Just over 3 million people live in the city of Athens – almost as many people as in the whole country of Albania.

More About . . .

The **Parthenon** temple in Athens is more than 2,400 years old. It was built in honour of the goddess Athena.

The **Valley of Roses** is a famous rose-growing area in Bulgaria. It also produces a rose oil used in perfumes.

The **Golden Kine** (or cows) are part of a gold treasure found in Bulgaria. It may be more than 6,000 years old!

Olives are the fruit of the olive tree. They are green when unripe and black when ripe.

Pelicans live around the Black Sea. This large bird uses the pouch attached to its bill to scoop up fish from the water.

Csikós are Hungarian cowboys who once worked on the Great Hungarian Plain. Today most perform in shows for tourists.

Bran Castle was built in 1377 to guard a pass over the Transylvanian Alps.

The Romans built a vast **amphitheatre**, seating thousands, at the port of Pula in Croatia.

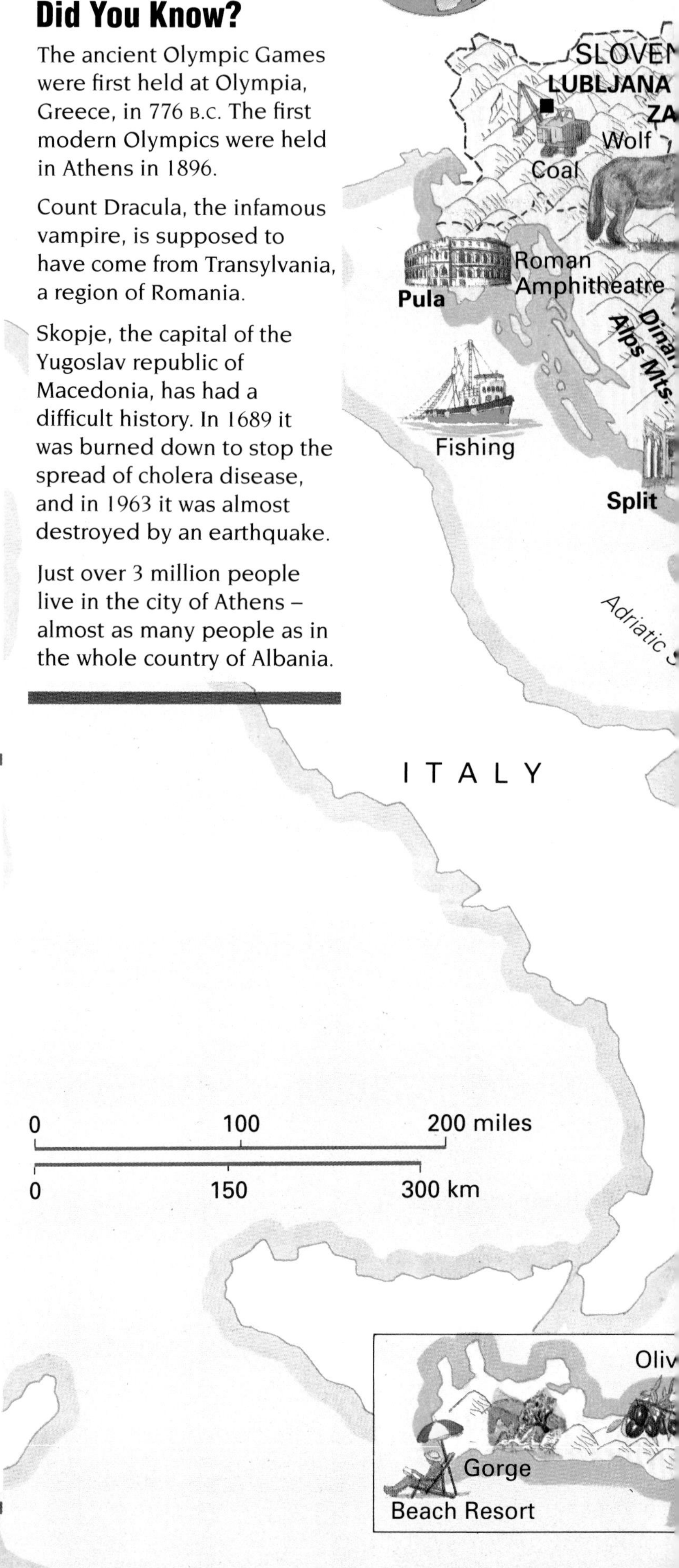
SLOVEN
LUBLJANA
ZA
Wolf
Coal
Roman Amphitheatre
Pula
Dinar. Alps Mts.
Fishing
Split
Adriatic S
ITALY
0 100 200 miles
0 150 300 km
Oliv
Gorge
Beach Resort

UKRAINE
MOLDAVIA
Timber
Coal
Lynx
Grapes
Sugar Beets
Rice
Apples
BUDAPEST
Csikós
apes
Pigs
Mining
Stork
Maize
NGARY
Danube
Wheat
Cluj-Napoca
Carpathian Mts.
Monastery
Beef Cattle
Sugar Beets
Wild Boar
Sunflowers
atoes
Grapes
Natural Gas
Paprika
Maize
Transylvanian Alps Mts.
Pelican
Drava
Apples
Bran Castle
ural Gas
Dairy Cattle
Timber
ROATIA
Pigs
Wheat
Pigs
Coal
Reeds
OSNIA AND ZEGOVINA
BELGRADE
Geese
Tobacco
ROMANIA
Skiing
Wheat
Grapes
Mining
Potatoes
Mining
BUCHAREST
Oil
SERBIA
Mining
Maize
Danube
Grapes
SARAJEVO
YUGOSLAVIA
Sugar Beets
Beach Resorts
Wheat
Wheat
Sunflowers
Brown Bear
BULGARIA
Roses
Golden Kine
Beach Resorts
MONTENEGRO
SOFIA
Black Sea
es
Coal
Balkan Mts.
ovnik
Barley
Timber
Grapes
Sheep
SKOPJE
MACEDONIA
Timber
Tobacco
Cotton
Goat
Sheep
Cotton
Fishing
TIRANË
Cattle
Tobacco
Greek Dancers
ALBANIA
Pindus Mts.
Grapes
Olives
Mount Olympus
Aegean Sea
CORFU
Figs
Citrus Fruits
Sheep
TURKEY
Ionian Sea
GREECE
Fishing
Olives
The Parthenon
Octopus
Corinth
ATHENS
Windmills
0
50 miles
0
75 km
Mining
Beach Resorts
Seaport
Olympia
Beach Resorts
ETE
Palm Tree
Silver
cient Ruins
RHODES

Beaufort Sea
QUEEN ELIZABETH ISLA
Fur Seal
Snow Goose
BANKS ISLAND
Walrus
Yukon
Arctic Fox
ALASKA
(U. S. A.)
Mining
VICTORIA ISLAND
Oil
Sea Otter
YUKON TERRITORY
Mackenzie
Snowy Owl
Oil
Anchorage
Great Bear Lake
NORTHWEST TERRITORIES
Rocky Mts.
Grizzly Bear
Oil Tanker
Inuit
Harlequin Duck
Moos
CANADA
Whitehorse
Juneau
Leaping Salmon
Yellowknife
Pacific Ocean
Mountain Goat
Oil
Dolphin
Great Slave Lake
Lake Athabasca
Salmon
BRITISH COLUMBIA
Pigs
ALBERTA
SASKATCHEWAN
Skiing
Edmonton
VANCOUVER ISLAND
Harvesting Wheat
Totem Pole
Rodeo
Fishing
Vancouver
Calgary
Wheat
Seaport
Regina
Winni

More About . . .

The **Inuit** people live in the Arctic. Some still hunt, but many work as fishermen or miners.

The **CN Tower** in Toronto is 361 metres high. It is made of steel and concrete and is the world's highest freestanding structure.

Lumberjacks cut down trees with power saws in Canada's forests. They can make the trees fall just where they want.

The **Royal Canadian Mounted Police** force rode on horseback until 1929. Today aircraft and snowmobiles are often used.

Did You Know?

Canada has two official languages: English and French. One quarter of the people speak French as their first language.

Fantastic shimmering flashes of light often brighten the arctic skies in the north of Canada. They are known as the aurora borealis, or the northern lights.

The world's largest exhibit of complete dinosaur skeletons can be found in a museum near the city of Calgary.

Canada

Canada is the second-largest country in the world. The far north is very cold – polar bears, arctic foxes and geese live in this icy world. To the south, the land is covered by great forests, which provide timber that is used to make furniture and paper. In the centre of Canada are the prairies – flat plains where wheat is grown. Splendid lakes teeming with fish are found in the Rocky Mountains in the west, and commercial fishing is an important export industry on Canada's east coast.

Most Canadians live in southern cities, around the Great Lakes and the St. Lawrence Seaway, where the weather is warmer.

Lemming
Baffin Bay
Inuit in Kayak
Seal
Arctic Hare
Polar Bear
Inuit
BAFFIN ISLAND
Hudson Strait
Narwhal
Flying Boat
Opossum
Hudson Bay
Caribou
Mining
Whale
Churchill
NEWFOUNDLAND
Fishing
St. John's
Ice Hockey
QUEBEC
TOBA
ONTARIO
Ice-breaking Ship
Winnipeg
Albany
Sugar Maple
Dairy Cattle
St. Lawrence
NEW BRUNSWICK
Fishing
Mounted Policeman
Apples
Quebec
Maize
Halifax
Montreal
Lumberjack
NOVA SCOTIA
Lake Superior
Atlantic Ocean
Beaver
0
250
500 miles
.A.
CN Tower
OTTAWA
0
400
800 km
Lake Huron
Toronto
Lake Ontario
Lake Michigan
Niagara Falls
Lake Erie

United States of America

The United States of America is made up of 50 states. Forty-eight lie between Canada to the north and Mexico to the south. The 49th and 50th states are separated from the others: Alaska is west of Canada, while Hawaii is southwest of the mainland in the Pacific Ocean.

The first Americans were Indians, who travelled from Asia in prehistoric times. Europeans began to arrive more than 400 years ago. Later, black Africans were brought to work as slaves – until slavery was ended in 1865. More recently, people from Asia and from Central and South America have moved to the U.S.A.

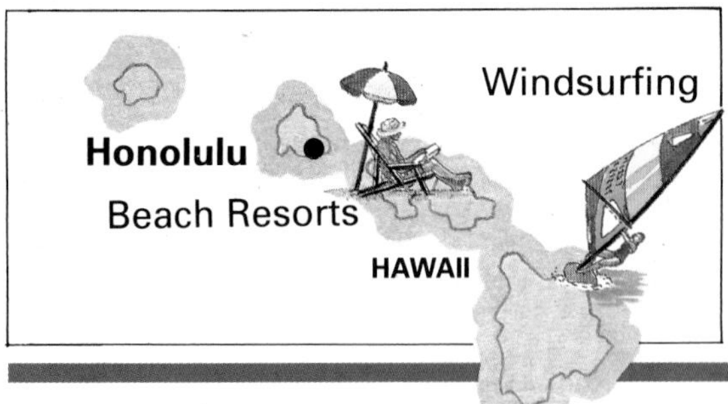

Honolulu
Beach Resorts
Windsurfing
HAWAII

CANADA
Apples
WASHINGTON
Columbia
Snake
Timber
OREGON
IDAHO
Mining
Natural Gas
MONTANA
Grizzly Bear
Geyser
Puma
NEVADA
Redwood Trees
Sierra Nevada Mts.
Bald Eagle
Rocky Mts.
WYOMING
CALIFORNIA
San Francisco
Grapes
UTAH
Mojave Indians
Skiing
COLORADO
Computer Industry
Oranges
Grand Canyon
ARIZONA
Los Angeles
Disneyland
Colorado
Mining
Saguaro Cactus
Pacific Ocean
MEXICO

More About . . .

Giant **redwood trees** grow in California. Some are more than 2,000 years old. The tallest is 110 metres high.

Old Faithful geyser in Yellowstone National Park shoots hot water and steam high into the air every hour.

The **Mojave Indians** were one of several tribes to settle in what is now California. Very few Indians live here today.

American football teams compete each year to try to win the Super Bowl trophy.

Huge herds of **buffalo** once roamed the western plains. Today only a few remain.

American **alligators**, once threatened, now live mainly in protected southern swamp areas.

Did You Know?

On the U.S. flag, the 50 stars stand for the 50 states. The stripes stand for the 13 original colonies.

The Grand Canyon is one of the natural wonders of the world. The cliffs tower over the Colorado River.

The first person to walk on the moon was an American astronaut, Neil A. Armstrong, in 1969.

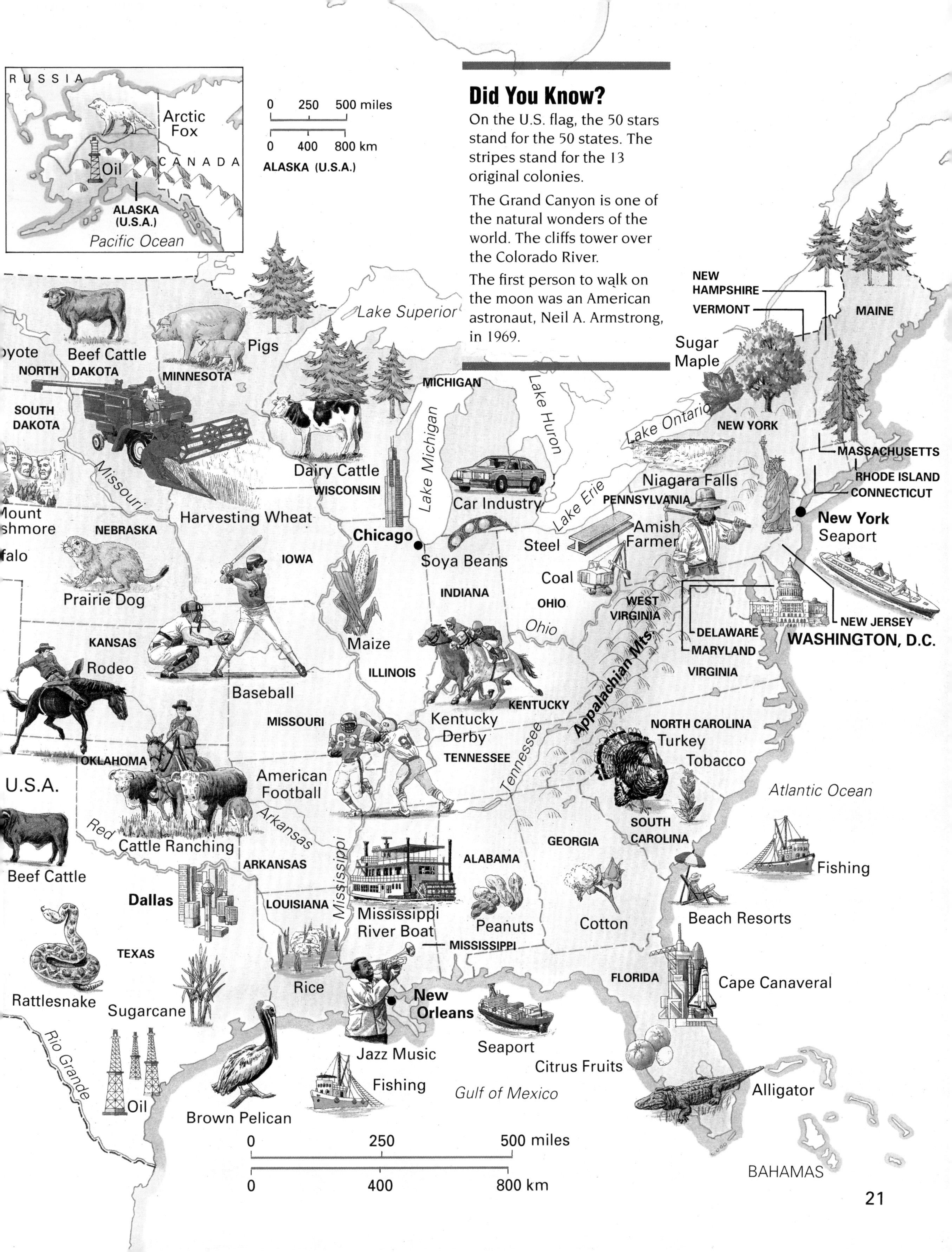

RUSSIA
Arctic Fox
Oil
CANADA
ALASKA (U.S.A.)
Pacific Ocean
0 250 500 miles
0 400 800 km
ALASKA (U.S.A.)
Lake Superior
Beef Cattle
Pigs
NORTH DAKOTA
MINNESOTA
SOUTH DAKOTA
MICHIGAN
Lake Michigan
Lake Huron
Lake Ontario
NEW HAMPSHIRE
VERMONT
MAINE
Sugar Maple
NEW YORK
MASSACHUSETTS
RHODE ISLAND
CONNECTICUT
Dairy Cattle
WISCONSIN
Missouri
Harvesting Wheat
Car Industry
Lake Erie
Niagara Falls
PENNSYLVANIA
Amish Farmer
New York Seaport
NEBRASKA
Chicago
Steel
IOWA
Soya Beans
Coal
Prairie Dog
INDIANA
OHIO
WEST VIRGINIA
NEW JERSEY
DELAWARE
MARYLAND
WASHINGTON, D.C.
Ohio
KANSAS
Maize
Rodeo
ILLINOIS
Appalachian Mts
VIRGINIA
Baseball
KENTUCKY
MISSOURI
Kentucky Derby
NORTH CAROLINA
Turkey
Tobacco
OKLAHOMA
TENNESSEE
Tennessee
U.S.A.
American Football
Atlantic Ocean
Red
Arkansas
Cattle Ranching
SOUTH CAROLINA
GEORGIA
Beef Cattle
ARKANSAS
Mississippi
ALABAMA
Fishing
Dallas
LOUISIANA
Mississippi River Boat
Peanuts
Cotton
Beach Resorts
MISSISSIPPI
TEXAS
FLORIDA
Cape Canaveral
Rice
Rattlesnake
Sugarcane
New Orleans
Rio Grande
Seaport
Jazz Music
Citrus Fruits
Fishing
Gulf of Mexico
Alligator
Oil
Brown Pelican
0 250 500 miles
0 400 800 km
BAHAMAS

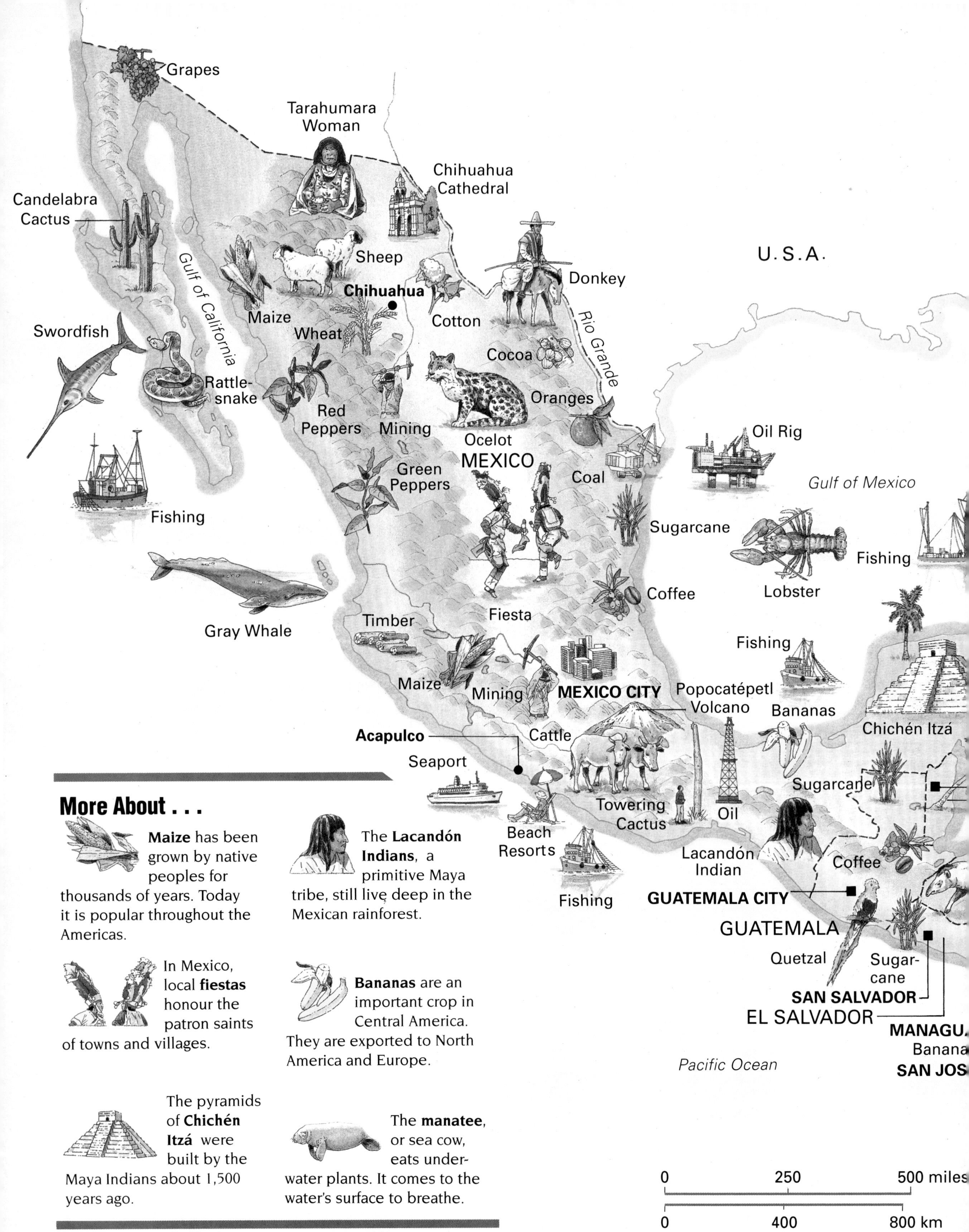
Grapes
Tarahumara Woman
Chihuahua Cathedral
Candelabra Cactus
U.S.A.
Gulf of California
Sheep
Donkey
Chihuahua
Maize
Wheat
Cotton
Rio Grande
Swordfish
Cocoa
Rattle-snake
Red Peppers
Mining
Oranges
Ocelot
MEXICO
Oil Rig
Gulf of Mexico
Green Peppers
Coal
Fishing
Sugarcane
Fishing
Lobster
Coffee
Gray Whale
Timber
Fiesta
Fishing
Maize
Mining
MEXICO CITY
Popocatépetl Volcano
Bananas
Chichén Itzá
Acapulco
Cattle
Seaport
Sugarcane
Towering Cactus
Oil
Beach Resorts
Lacandón Indian
Coffee
Fishing
GUATEMALA CITY
GUATEMALA
Quetzal
Sugar-cane
SAN SALVADOR
EL SALVADOR
MANAGU
Banana
SAN JOS
Pacific Ocean
0
250
500 miles
0
400
800 km

More About . . .

Maize has been grown by native peoples for thousands of years. Today it is popular throughout the Americas.

In Mexico, local **fiestas** honour the patron saints of towns and villages.

The pyramids of **Chichén Itzá** were built by the Maya Indians about 1,500 years ago.

The **Lacandón Indians**, a primitive Maya tribe, still live deep in the Mexican rainforest.

Bananas are an important crop in Central America. They are exported to North America and Europe.

The **manatee**, or sea cow, eats under-water plants. It comes to the water's surface to breathe.

Mexico, Central America and the Caribbean

Mexico is on the North American continent, as are the 7 countries of Central America. These countries form a land bridge between Mexico and South America. People of this area are descendants of the Indians who originally lived here and the Europeans who came more than 400 years ago.

The Caribbean islands stretch in an arc across the Caribbean Sea. These islands were once ruled by other countries, but today most of them are independent. Many Caribbean people are descended from African slaves who were brought to work on the sugar plantations there.

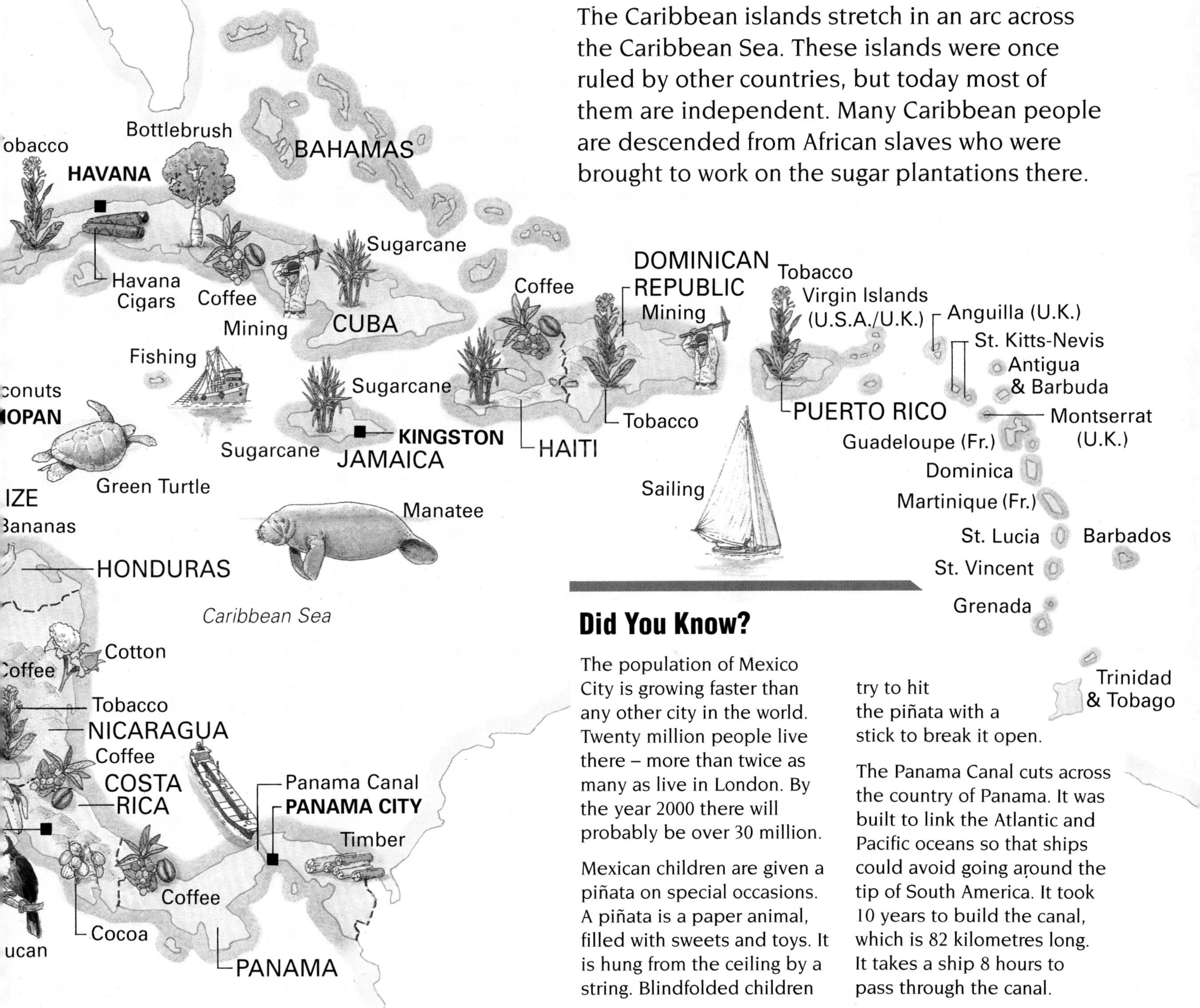

Bottlebrush
obacco
HAVANA
BAHAMAS
Sugarcane
Havana Cigars
Coffee
Mining
CUBA
Fishing
conuts
OPAN
Sugarcane
KINGSTON
Sugarcane
JAMAICA
Green Turtle
IZE
3ananas
Manatee
HONDURAS
Caribbean Sea
Cotton
offee
Tobacco
NICARAGUA
Coffee
COSTA RICA
Panama Canal
PANAMA CITY
Timber
Coffee
Cocoa
ucan
PANAMA
Coffee
DOMINICAN REPUBLIC
Mining
Tobacco
HAITI
Tobacco
Virgin Islands (U.S.A./U.K.)
Anguilla (U.K.)
St. Kitts-Nevis
Antigua & Barbuda
PUERTO RICO
Montserrat (U.K.)
Guadeloupe (Fr.)
Dominica
Sailing
Martinique (Fr.)
St. Lucia
Barbados
St. Vincent
Grenada
Trinidad & Tobago

Did You Know?

The population of Mexico City is growing faster than any other city in the world. Twenty million people live there – more than twice as many as live in London. By the year 2000 there will probably be over 30 million.

Mexican children are given a piñata on special occasions. A piñata is a paper animal, filled with sweets and toys. It is hung from the ceiling by a string. Blindfolded children try to hit the piñata with a stick to break it open.

The Panama Canal cuts across the country of Panama. It was built to link the Atlantic and Pacific oceans so that ships could avoid going around the tip of South America. It took 10 years to build the canal, which is 82 kilometres long. It takes a ship 8 hours to pass through the canal.

South America: North

The landscape of this region varies from the high Andes Mountains and desert in the west to thick rainforest in the north and east. The Andes, which run down the west coast of South America, are rich in minerals, such as silver, zinc and iron. The River Amazon begins high in the mountains of Peru and flows across Brazil. It is fed by hundreds of small rivers in Peru, Bolivia, Ecuador, Colombia, and Venezuela.

Highlands stretch across Venezuela into Guyana, Suriname and French Guiana. The highlands are mainly rainforest, with small areas of grassland. Venezuela is the richest country in the region. It is one of the world's major oil producers.

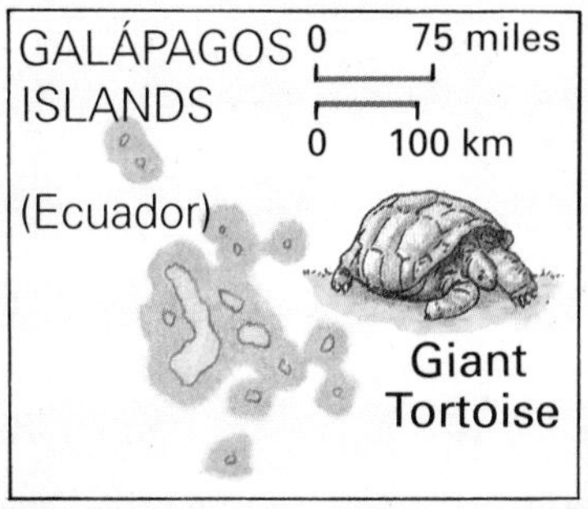
GALÁPAGOS ISLANDS
(Ecuador)
0 75 miles
0 100 km
Giant Tortoise

The first people in South America were American Indians. Today its people are descendants of American Indians and of the Europeans who settled there more than 450 years ago.

More About . . .

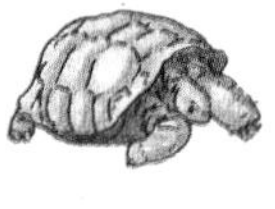

Giant tortoises live on the Galápagos Islands in the Pacific Ocean. They grow up to 1.5 metres long and can weigh 159 kilograms. Today they are an endangered species.

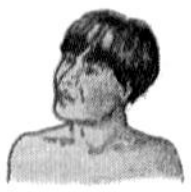

The surviving **Cuiva Indians** live in small groups on the plains of Colombia. Every four weeks they move camp. They hunt wild pigs, catch fish and gather fruit.

Armadillo means 'little armoured one' in Spanish. It has hard plates covering its back and sides. This burrowing animal curls up in a ball when it senses danger.

Panama hats are famous all over the world. They are made from leaves of the palm-like jipijapa plant, which grows in Ecuador.

The ruins of the ancient Inca city of **Machu Picchu** were found in 1911. Today it is one of Peru's most popular tourist sites.

Angel Falls, in Venezuela, is the world's highest waterfall. The water plunges over 975 metres into the river below.

The **condor** is a huge bird that is part of the vulture family. The condor soars high over the Andes. It has a wingspan of 3 metres.

The **Aymara Indians** live high in the Andes Mountains. They fish on Lake Titicaca – their boats are made from lakeshore reeds.

Cayenne pepper is bright red and very hot! It is a spice that comes from a plant grown around Cayenne, the capital of French Guiana.

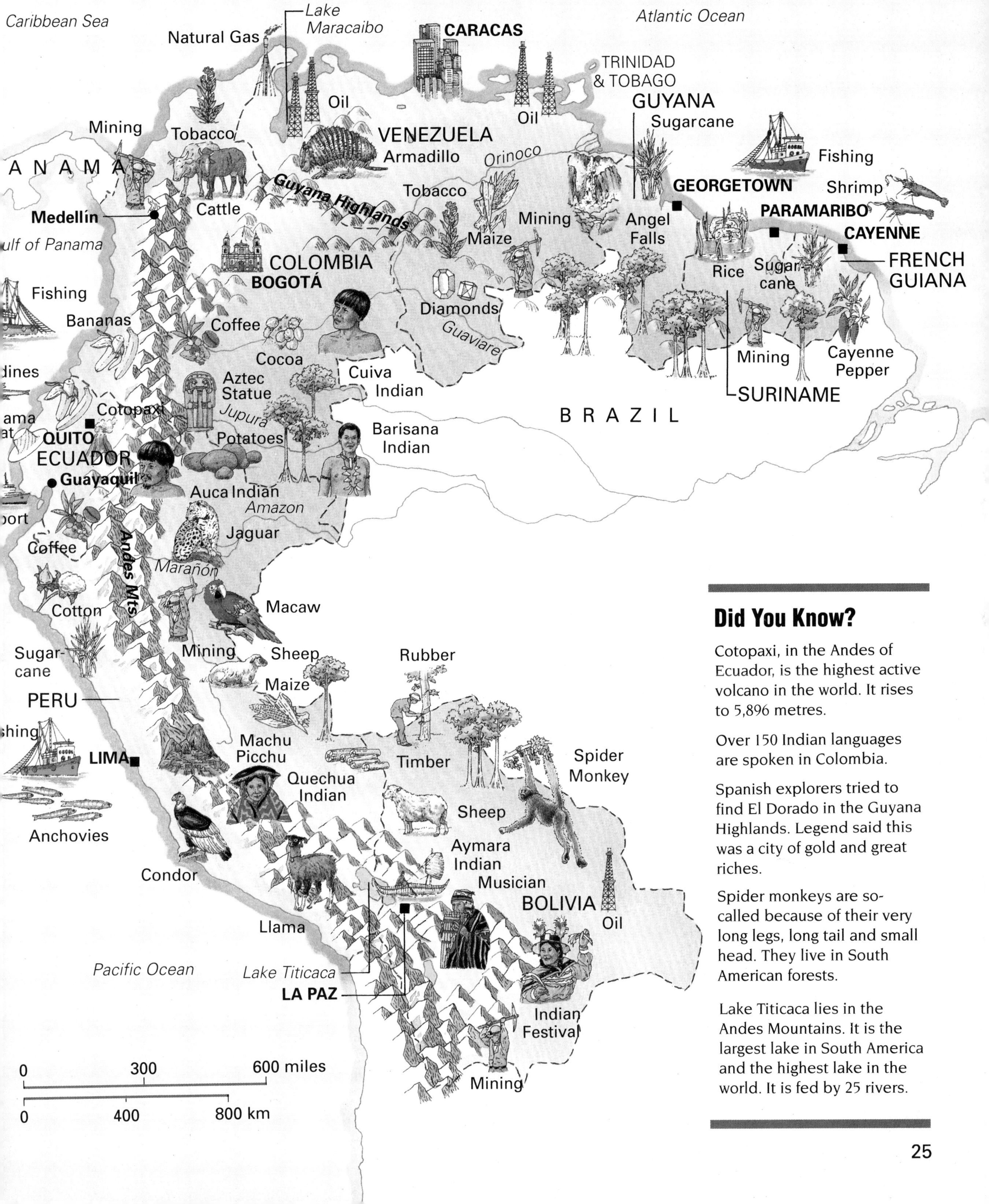
Caribbean Sea
Natural Gas
Lake Maracaibo
CARACAS
Atlantic Ocean
TRINIDAD & TOBAGO
GUYANA
Sugarcane
Oil
Oil
Mining
Tobacco
VENEZUELA
Armadillo
Orinoco
Fishing
ANAMA
Medellín
Cattle
Guyana Highlands
Tobacco
GEORGETOWN
Shrimp
PARAMARIBO
Mining
Angel Falls
Maize
CAYENNE
ulf of Panama
COLOMBIA
BOGOTÁ
Rice
Sugar-cane
FRENCH GUIANA
Fishing
Diamonds
Bananas
Coffee
Guaviare
Mining
Cayenne Pepper
Cocoa
dines
Cuiva Indian
SURINAME
Aztec Statue
Cotopaxi
BRAZIL
Jupura
QUITO
Potatoes
Barisana Indian
ECUADOR
Guayaquil
Auca Indian
Amazon
Jaguar
Coffee
Andes Mts
Marañon
Macaw
Cotton
Rubber
Sugar-cane
Mining
Sheep
Maize
PERU
Machu Picchu
LIMA
Timber
Spider Monkey
Quechua Indian
Sheep
Anchovies
Aymara Indian
Condor
Musician
BOLIVIA
Oil
Llama
Pacific Ocean
Lake Titicaca
LA PAZ
Indian Festival
Mining
0
300
600 miles
0
400
800 km

Did You Know?

Cotopaxi, in the Andes of Ecuador, is the highest active volcano in the world. It rises to 5,896 metres.

Over 150 Indian languages are spoken in Colombia.

Spanish explorers tried to find El Dorado in the Guyana Highlands. Legend said this was a city of gold and great riches.

Spider monkeys are so-called because of their very long legs, long tail and small head. They live in South American forests.

Lake Titicaca lies in the Andes Mountains. It is the largest lake in South America and the highest lake in the world. It is fed by 25 rivers.

South America: Brazil

Brazil is the largest country in South America. It contains the biggest tropical rainforest in the world. The River Amazon runs through the hot, steamy terrain. Some Indian tribes still live here.

The main cities of Brazil are in the south of the country. São Paulo is the largest city. Rio de Janeiro, famed for its beaches, is known for its annual carnival. In 1960, the newly built city of Brasília became Brazil's capital.

Did You Know?

So much rain falls in the Amazon region that Brazilians divide the seasons into times of 'big rains' and 'little rains'.

Over 1,000 types of fish live in the Amazon.

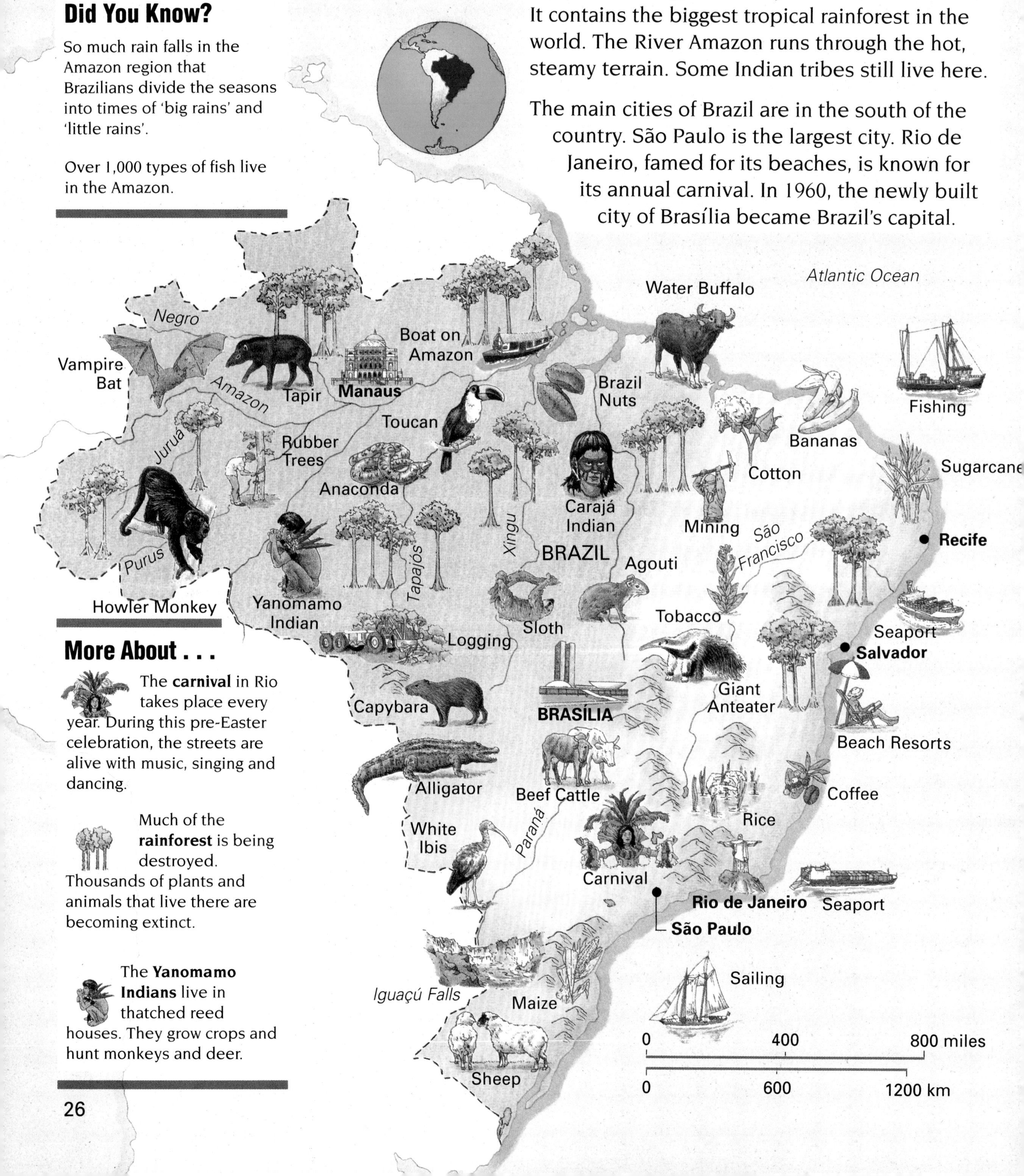

Atlantic Ocean
Water Buffalo
Negro
Vampire Bat
Amazon
Tapir
Manaus
Boat on Amazon
Brazil Nuts
Fishing
Bananas
Toucan
Juruá
Rubber Trees
Anaconda
Cotton
Sugarcane
Carajá Indian
Mining
São Francisco
Recife
Purus
Xingu
Tapajós
BRAZIL
Agouti
Howler Monkey
Yanomamo Indian
Logging
Sloth
Tobacco
Seaport
Salvador
Giant Anteater
Capybara
BRASÍLIA
Beach Resorts
Alligator
Beef Cattle
Coffee
White Ibis
Paraná
Rice
Carnival
Rio de Janeiro
Seaport
São Paulo
Sailing
Iguaçú Falls
Maize
Sheep
0
400
800 miles
0
600
1200 km

More About . . .

The **carnival** in Rio takes place every year. During this pre-Easter celebration, the streets are alive with music, singing and dancing.

Much of the **rainforest** is being destroyed. Thousands of plants and animals that live there are becoming extinct.

The **Yanomamo Indians** live in thatched reed houses. They grow crops and hunt monkeys and deer.

South America: South

The Andes Mountains continue south through Chile and Argentina. They stretch to the tip of the South American continent. The Andes dominate Chile, which is a long, narrow country on the Pacific coast. To the east are vast areas of grassland in Argentina, Paraguay and Uruguay. Cattle and sheep graze here. Wheat and maize grow on the pampas – flat, treeless plains in Argentina. In the south, there are big reserves of oil and gas. The weather is often cold, and there are lakes, waterfalls and volcanoes.

As in the rest of South America, the people of these countries are descended mainly from American Indians and Spanish settlers. Most people live in big cities. The capitals of Argentina, Chile and Uruguay are each home to over a third of their country's people.

BOLIVIA
Guaraní Indian
Prickly Pear Cactus
BRAZIL
Fishing
PARAGUAY
Volcano
Cotton
Antofagasta
Beef Cattle
ASUNCIÓN
Mining
Timber
CHILE
Sugarcane
Andes Mts
Football
Knitwear
Pacific Ocean
Maize
URUGUAY
Seaport
Grapes
Citrus Fruits
SANTIAGO
Sheep
Wheat
MONTEVIDEO
ARGENTINA
Pampas
Fishing
Mining
Torrent Duck
BUENOS AIRES
Seaport
Dairy Cattle
Beef Cattle
Gaucho
Penguin
Atlantic Ocean
Guanaco
Oil
Monkey Puzzle Tree
Killer Whale
Sheep
FALKLAND ISLANDS (U.K.)
Oil
Penguin
Fur Seal
TIERRA DEL FUEGO

Did You Know?

The Tierra del Fuego islands are shared by two countries. The western islands belong to Chile, and the eastern islands belong to Argentina.

Many interesting animals live in the Andes Mountains. Some of these are llamas, guanacos, alpacas, and vicuñas. They are all members of the camel family.

Penguins live on the southern shores of Chile and Argentina. They also live on the Falkland Islands.

Monkey puzzle trees grow in Chile and Argentina. They got their name because it is said even monkeys find them hard to climb.

More About . . .

The **prickly pear cactus** grows in the deserts of North and South America. It bears a pear-like fruit covered in thorns.

Gauchos are Argentinian cowboys. They herd cattle on the grassy plains called pampas.

Football is the national sport in South America. Argentina and Uruguay have each won the World Cup twice.

The **Andes** form the longest mountain chain in the world, stretching for 7,401 kilometres.

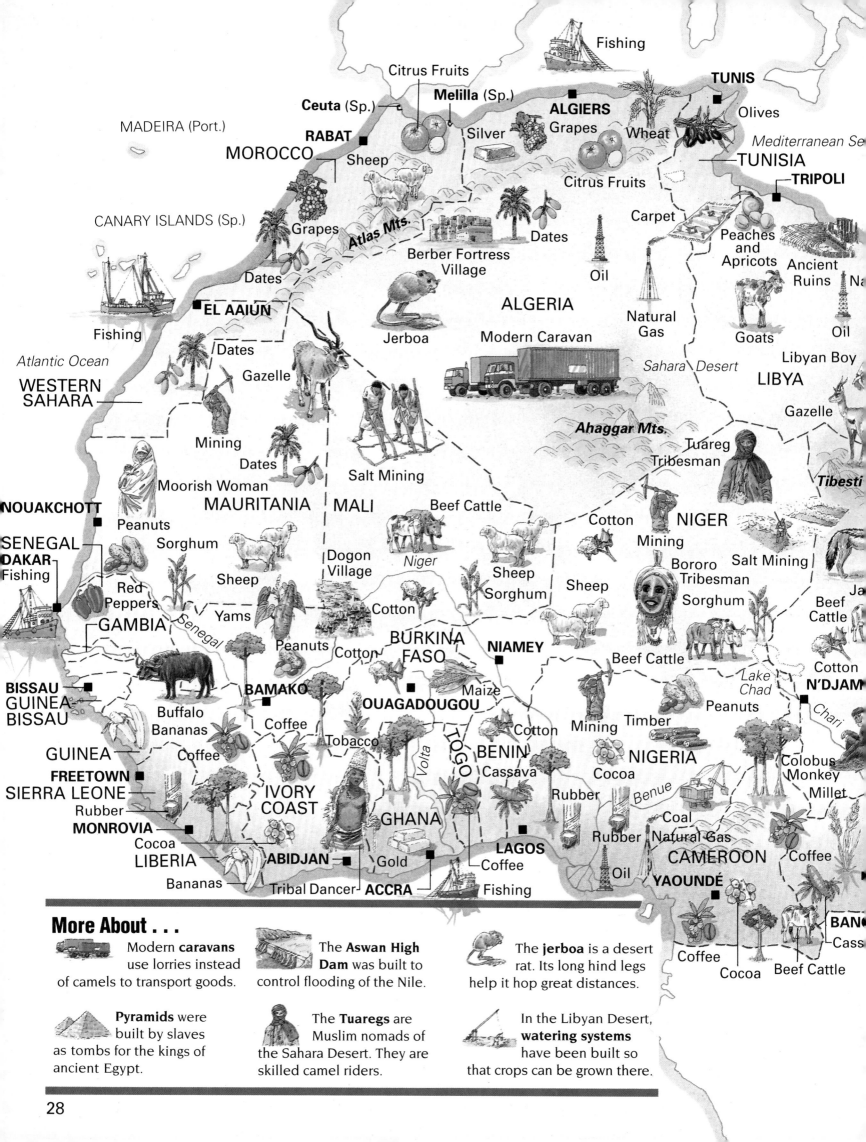

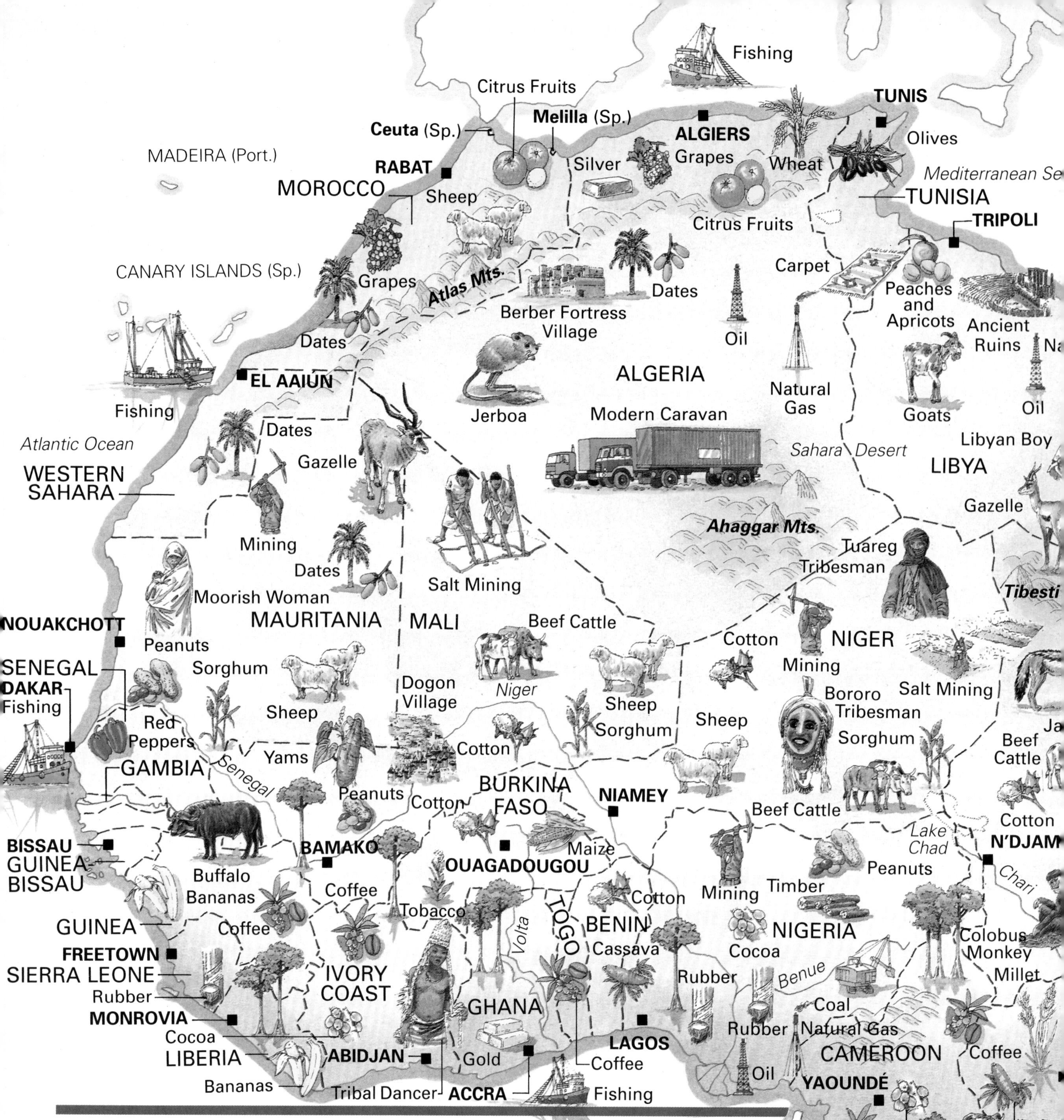
Fishing
Citrus Fruits
TUNIS
Ceuta (Sp.)
Melilla (Sp.)
ALGIERS
Olives
MADEIRA (Port.)
RABAT
Silver
Grapes
Wheat
Mediterranean Se
MOROCCO
Sheep
TUNISIA
TRIPOLI
Citrus Fruits
CANARY ISLANDS (Sp.)
Carpet
Grapes
Atlas Mts.
Dates
Peaches and Apricots
Berber Fortress Village
Ancient Ruins
Dates
Oil
Fishing
EL AAIUN
ALGERIA
Natural Gas
Goats
Oil
Jerboa
Modern Caravan
Dates
Libyan Boy
Atlantic Ocean
Gazelle
Sahara Desert
LIBYA
WESTERN SAHARA
Gazelle
Ahaggar Mts.
Mining
Tuareg Tribesman
Dates
Salt Mining
Tibesti
Moorish Woman
MAURITANIA
MALI
Beef Cattle
NOUAKCHOTT
Cotton
NIGER
Peanuts
Mining
SENEGAL
Sorghum
Dogon Village
Niger
Bororo Tribesman
Salt Mining
DAKAR
Fishing
Sheep
Sheep
Sheep
Red Peppers
Sorghum
Sorghum
Beef Cattle
Yams
Cotton
GAMBIA
Senegal
BURKINA FASO
NIAMEY
Beef Cattle
Peanuts
Cotton
Cotton
Lake Chad
BISSAU
BAMAKO
Maize
N'DJAM
GUINEA-BISSAU
OUAGADOUGOU
Peanuts
Buffalo
Chari
Bananas
Coffee
Cotton
Mining
Timber
Tobacco
TOGO
GUINEA
Coffee
BENIN
NIGERIA
Volta
Colobus Monkey
FREETOWN
Cassava
Cocoa
SIERRA LEONE
IVORY COAST
Rubber
Benue
Millet
Rubber
GHANA
Coal
MONROVIA
Rubber
Natural Gas
Cocoa
LAGOS
CAMEROON
Coffee
LIBERIA
ABIDJAN
Gold
Coffee
Oil
YAOUNDÉ
Bananas
Tribal Dancer
ACCRA
Fishing
Coffee
Cocoa
Beef Cattle
Cass
BAN

More About . . .

Modern **caravans** use lorries instead of camels to transport goods.

The **Aswan High Dam** was built to control flooding of the Nile.

The **jerboa** is a desert rat. Its long hind legs help it hop great distances.

Pyramids were built by slaves as tombs for the kings of ancient Egypt.

The **Tuaregs** are Muslim nomads of the Sahara Desert. They are skilled camel riders.

In the Libyan Desert, **watering systems** have been built so that crops can be grown there.

Africa: North

The vast Sahara Desert stretches across north Africa. It is the largest desert in the world and covers all or part of 12 countries. Egypt is located on the east coast of Africa. Most Egyptians live on the 16-kilometre-wide oasis of the River Nile between Aswan and Cairo and in the delta below Cairo. The Nile flows from central Africa to the Mediterranean Sea. The river's name changes from country to country. The Blue Nile begins on the highlands of Ethiopia, joining the White Nile in Sudan. In both Egypt and Ethiopia, lack of rain and crop failures have caused terrible shortages of food, or famines.

On the west coast of Africa, the situation is different. In Nigeria, oil production started in the 1950s, and the money has been used to build roads, schools and hospitals. The coast of Cameroon, which borders Nigeria, is a swamp. The southern part of Cameroon is a rainforest.

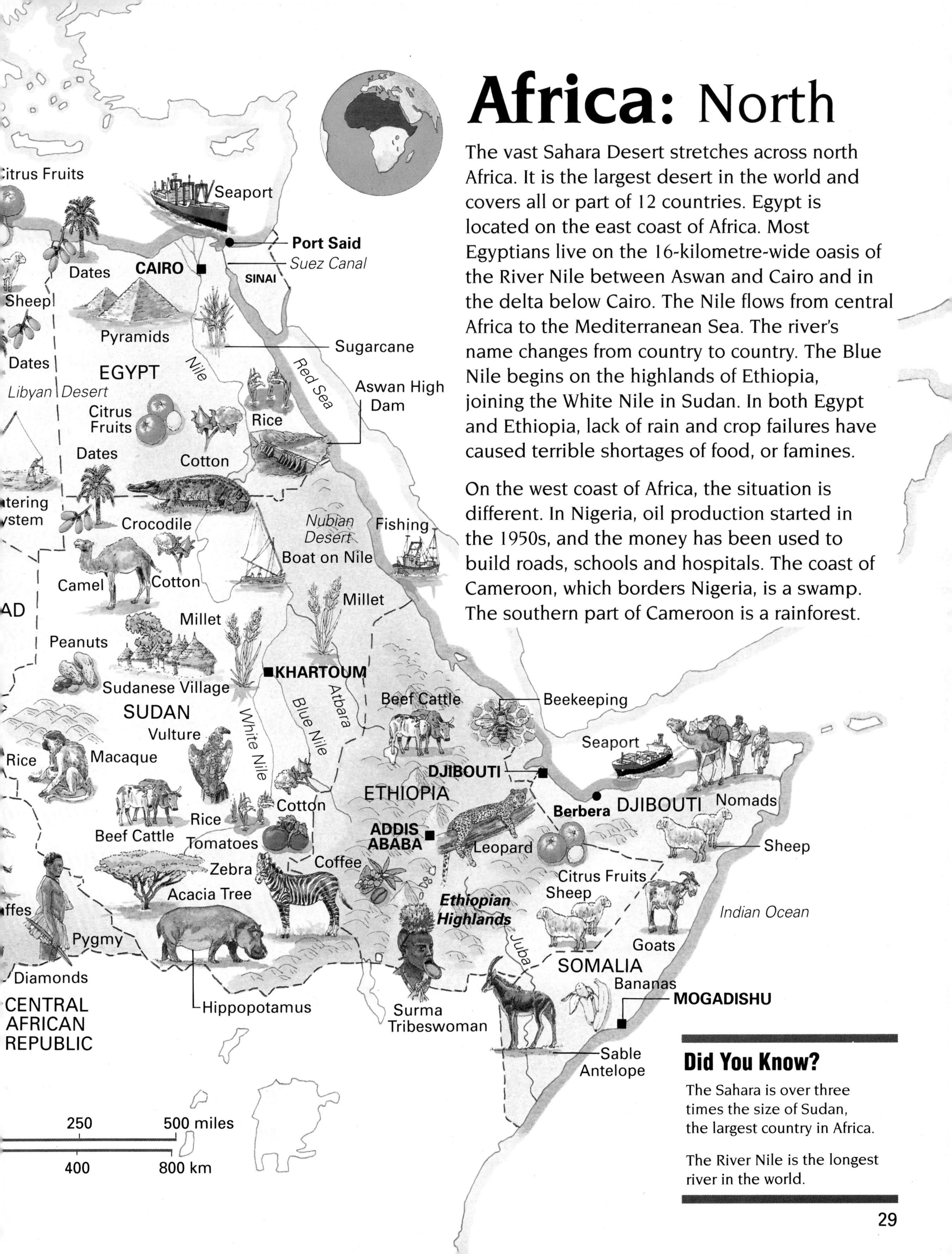

Citrus Fruits
Seaport
Port Said
Suez Canal
Dates
CAIRO
SINAI
Sheep
Pyramids
Sugarcane
Dates
EGYPT
Nile
Red Sea
Libyan Desert
Aswan High Dam
Citrus Fruits
Rice
Dates
Cotton
tering
ystem
Crocodile
Nubian Desert
Fishing
Boat on Nile
Camel
Cotton
Millet
AD
Millet
Peanuts
KHARTOUM
Sudanese Village
Atbara
Blue Nile
Beef Cattle
Beekeeping
SUDAN
White Nile
Vulture
Seaport
Rice
Macaque
DJIBOUTI
ETHIOPIA
Cotton
Berbera
DJIBOUTI
Nomads
Rice
ADDIS ABABA
Beef Cattle
Tomatoes
Leopard
Sheep
Zebra
Coffee
Citrus Fruits
Sheep
Acacia Tree
Ethiopian Highlands
ffes
Indian Ocean
Pygmy
Juba
Goats
SOMALIA
Diamonds
Bananas
MOGADISHU
CENTRAL AFRICAN REPUBLIC
Hippopotamus
Surma Tribeswoman
Sable Antelope
250
500 miles
400
800 km

Did You Know?

The Sahara is over three times the size of Sudan, the largest country in Africa.

The River Nile is the longest river in the world.

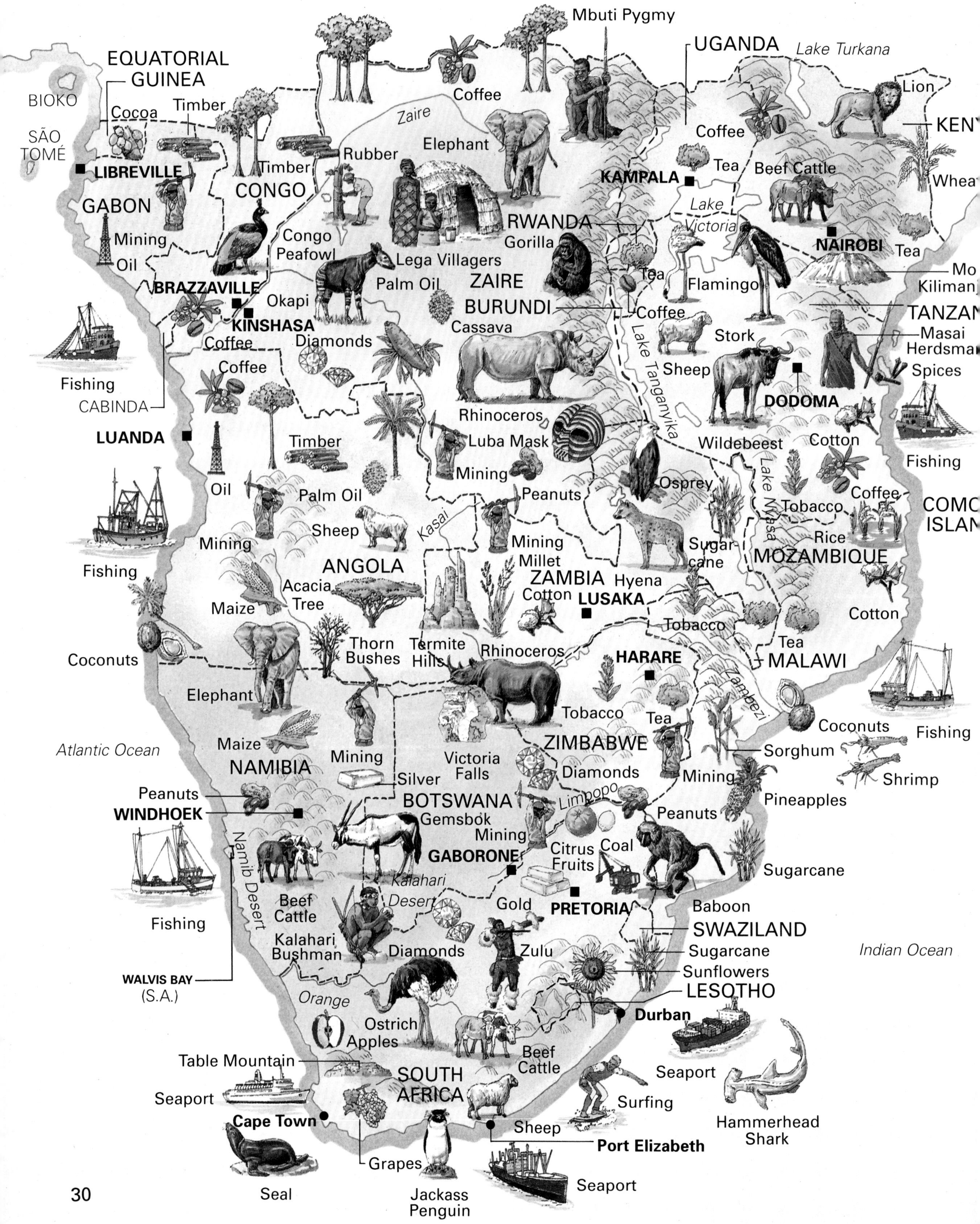
EQUATORIAL
GUINEA
BIOKO
SÃO
TOMÉ
Cocoa
Timber
Mbuti Pygmy
Coffee
UGANDA
Lake Turkana
Lion
KEN
Zaire
Elephant
Rubber
Timber
LIBREVILLE
CONGO
GABON
Coffee
Tea
Beef Cattle
Whea
KAMPALA
Lake
Victoria
RWANDA
Gorilla
NAIROBI
Tea
Mining
Oil
Congo
Peafowl
Lega Villagers
Tea
Flamingo
Mo
Kiliman
BRAZZAVILLE
Palm Oil
ZAIRE
Okapi
BURUNDI
Coffee
TANZAN
KINSHASA
Cassava
Masai
Herdsma
Coffee
Diamonds
Lake Tanganyika
Stork
Fishing
Coffee
Sheep
Spices
CABINDA
DODOMA
Rhinoceros
LUANDA
Luba Mask
Wildebeest
Cotton
Timber
Fishing
Mining
Osprey
Oil
Palm Oil
Peanuts
Coffee
Lake Nyasa
Tobacco
COMO
ISLAN
Sheep
Kasai
Mining
Sugar-
cane
Rice
Mining
Millet
MOZAMBIQUE
Fishing
ANGOLA
ZAMBIA
Hyena
Acacia
Tree
Cotton
LUSAKA
Maize
Cotton
Tobacco
Thorn
Bushes
Termite
Hills
Rhinoceros
Tea
Coconuts
HARARE
MALAWI
Zambezi
Elephant
Tobacco
Tea
Coconuts
Fishing
Atlantic Ocean
Maize
ZIMBABWE
Sorghum
NAMIBIA
Mining
Victoria
Falls
Diamonds
Shrimp
Silver
Mining
Peanuts
BOTSWANA
Limpopo
Pineapples
WINDHOEK
Gemsbok
Peanuts
Mining
Citrus
Fruits
Coal
Namib Desert
GABORONE
Sugarcane
Kalahari
Desert
Fishing
Beef
Cattle
Gold
PRETORIA
Baboon
SWAZILAND
Kalahari
Bushman
Diamonds
Zulu
Sugarcane
Indian Ocean
WALVIS BAY
(S.A.)
Sunflowers
LESOTHO
Orange
Durban
Ostrich
Apples
Beef
Cattle
Table Mountain
SOUTH
AFRICA
Seaport
Seaport
Surfing
Hammerhead
Shark
Cape Town
Sheep
Port Elizabeth
Grapes
Seal
Jackass
Penguin
Seaport

Africa: South

Tropical rainforests are found across the south of Africa. The River Zaire, also called the Congo, flows through the country of Zaire on its journey to the Atlantic Ocean. To the east, Kenya and Tanzania are famous for their wildlife. Antelopes, zebras, giraffes, elephants and rhinoceroses live on the savanna, a flat grassland. Snowcapped Mount Kilimanjaro, in Tanzania, is Africa's highest mountain. Farther south are the Kalahari Desert and the smaller Namib Desert.

Most southern African countries are rich in minerals. Zimbabwe has large deposits of copper, iron and gold. In South Africa, coal and the most precious gems – diamonds – are mined. The largest white European population on the continent is found in South Africa. In 1994 the 'apartheid' system, which had kept the black majority population separate and unequal, was abolished and a new government that was chosen by all the people was put in place.

The island of Madagascar lies to the east, in the Indian Ocean. Most of its people are farmers.

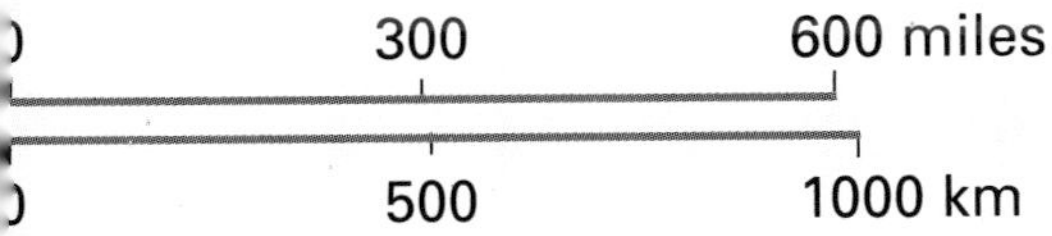
300
600 miles
500
1000 km

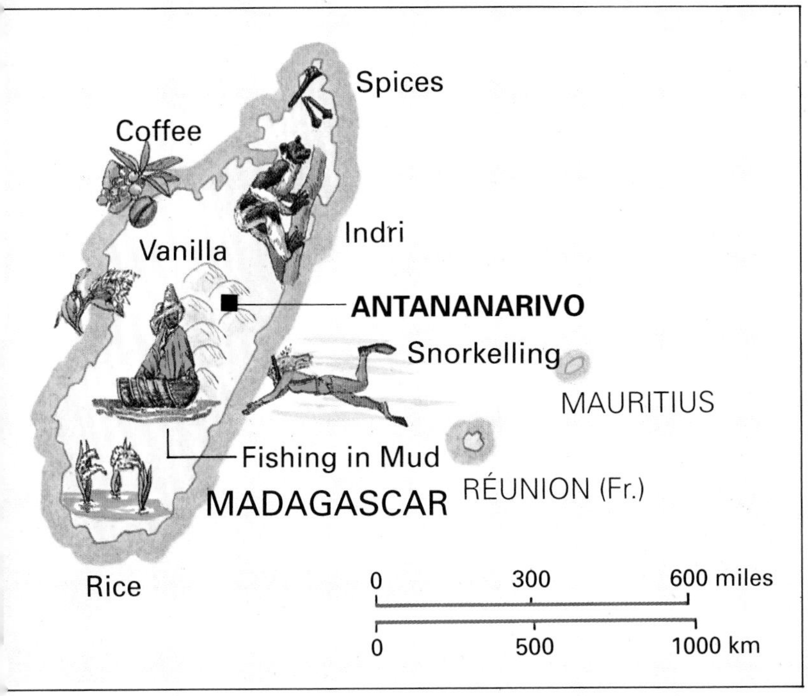
Spices
Coffee
Indri
Vanilla
ANTANANARIVO
Snorkelling
MAURITIUS
Fishing in Mud
RÉUNION (Fr.)
MADAGASCAR
Rice
0
300
600 miles
0
500
1000 km

More About . . .

The **Mbuti pygmies** of Zaire are the smallest people in the world. Their average height is 1.4 metres.

Gorillas live in some African rainforests. They look fierce, but are not dangerous unless attacked.

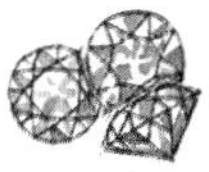

Miners blast or dig out rocks containing **diamonds**. The gems are then separated from gravel and other rock fragments.

Like bees, termites live in groups called colonies. **Termite hills** are the giant nests that termite colonies make from mounds of earth.

The **Kalahari bushmen** roam the desert. The women collect roots and berries, while the men hunt.

Zulus are the largest group of black Africans in South Africa. Many now work in the cities.

The spectacular **Victoria Falls**, of the Zambezi River, plunge 107 metres into a giant gorge below.

The **osprey**, or fish hawk, lives near lakes and rivers. It catches fish with its long claws.

The tall **Masai** live on the grasslands of Kenya and Tanzania. They are cattle herders.

The **rhinoceros** is usually calm. However, when it is threatened, the rhinoceros can charge at 50 kilometres per hour.

Did You Know?

The Watusi live in Rwanda and Burundi. They are among the tallest people in the world. The average height for men is nearly 2 metres.

In 1867, children playing beside the Orange River found the first South African diamond. A few years later there was a diamond rush, and the world-famous Kimberley mines opened.

Diamonds are harder than any other natural substance. Many are used in industry as parts of cutting tools.

Former Soviet Union

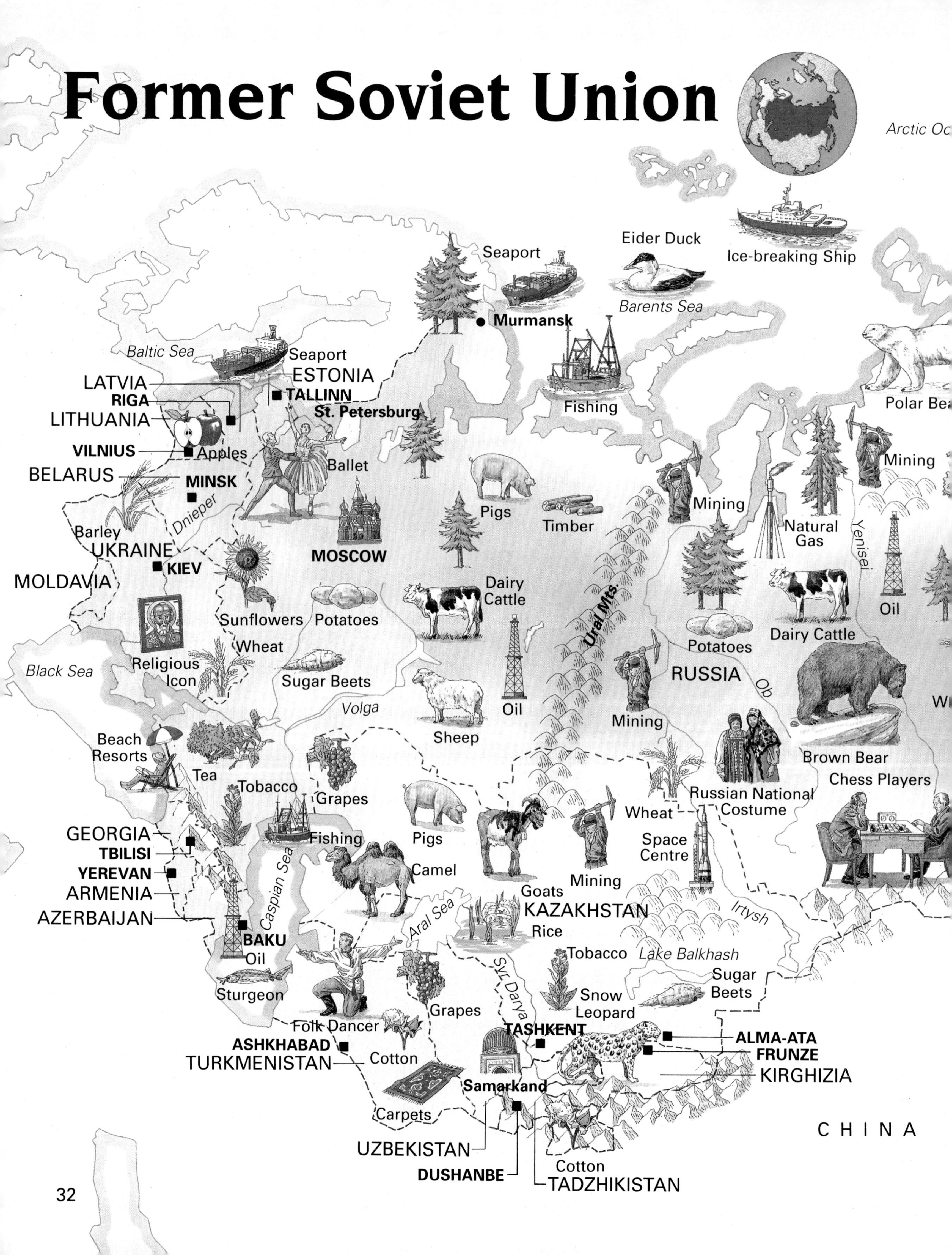

Arctic Oc
Eider Duck
Ice-breaking Ship
Seaport
Barents Sea
Murmansk
Baltic Sea
Seaport
LATVIA
RIGA
LITHUANIA
ESTONIA
TALLINN
St. Petersburg
Fishing
Polar Bea
VILNIUS
Apples
BELARUS
MINSK
Ballet
Pigs
Timber
Mining
Mining
Natural Gas
Yenisei
Dnieper
Barley
UKRAINE
KIEV
MOLDAVIA
MOSCOW
Dairy Cattle
Ural Mts.
Oil
Dairy Cattle
Sunflowers
Potatoes
Potatoes
Wheat
Religious Icon
Black Sea
Sugar Beets
Oil
RUSSIA
Ob
W
Volga
Sheep
Mining
Beach Resorts
Tea
Brown Bear
Chess Players
Tobacco
Grapes
Pigs
Wheat
Russian National Costume
GEORGIA
TBILISI
YEREVAN
ARMENIA
AZERBAIJAN
Fishing
Caspian Sea
Camel
Goats
Mining
Space Centre
KAZAKHSTAN
Irtysh
Aral Sea
BAKU
Oil
Rice
Tobacco
Lake Balkhash
Sugar Beets
Sturgeon
Grapes
Syr Darya
Snow Leopard
Folk Dancer
TASHKENT
ALMA-ATA
ASHKHABAD
FRUNZE
TURKMENISTAN
Cotton
KIRGHIZIA
Samarkand
Carpets
CHINA
UZBEKISTAN
DUSHANBE
Cotton
TADZHIKISTAN

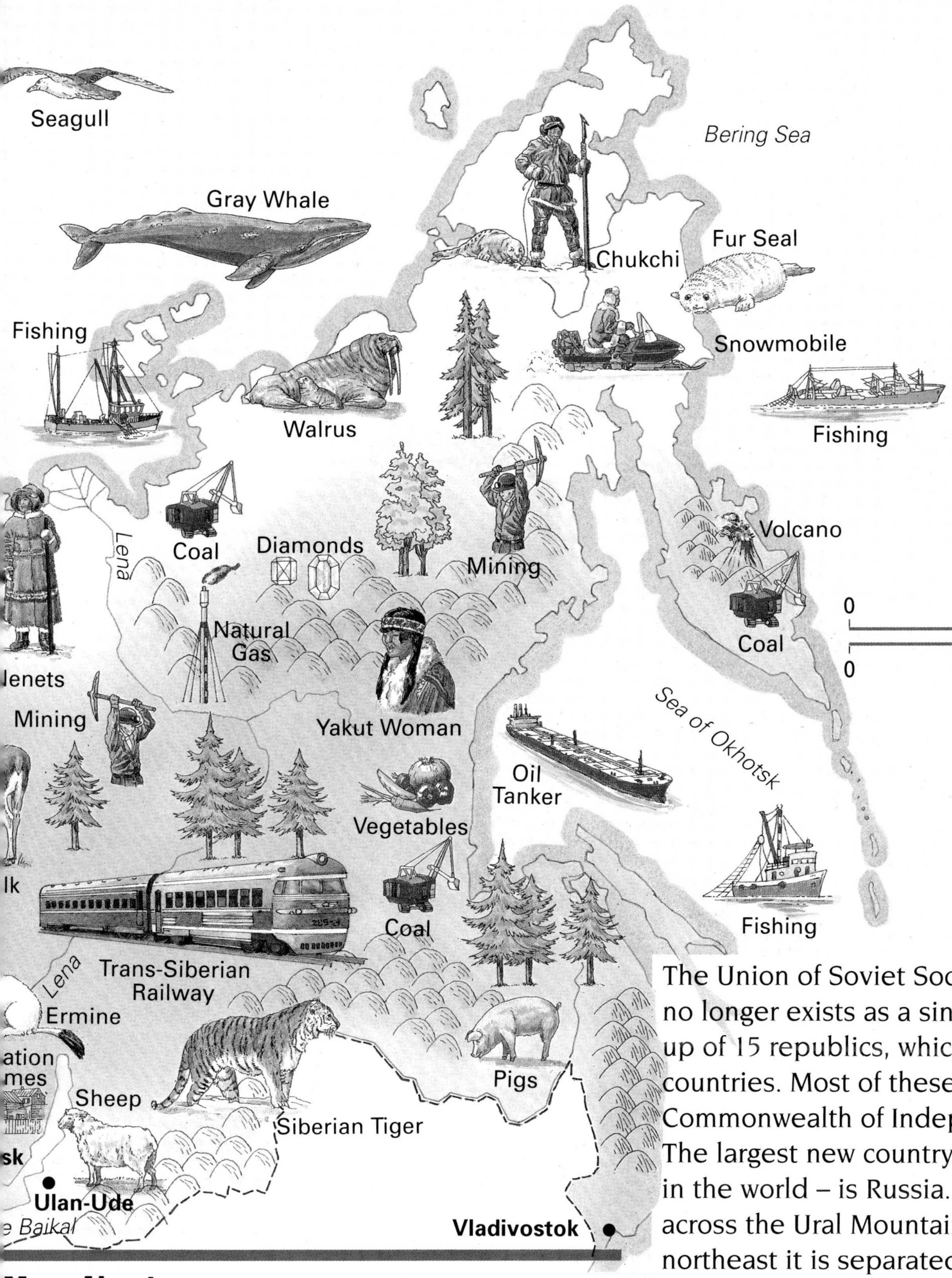
Seagull
Gray Whale
Bering Sea
Chukchi
Fur Seal
Fishing
Snowmobile
Walrus
Fishing
Volcano
Lena
Coal
Diamonds
Mining
Natural Gas
Coal
0
400
800 miles
0
600
1200 km
lenets
Mining
Yakut Woman
Sea of Okhotsk
Oil Tanker
Vegetables
lk
Coal
Fishing
Lena
Trans-Siberian Railway
Ermine
ation
mes
Sheep
Pigs
Siberian Tiger
sk
Ulan-Ude
e Baikal
Vladivostok

Did You Know?

A Russian named Yuri Gagarin was the first man in space in 1961. The first woman in space was also Russian, Valentina Tereshkova, in 1963.

Many chess champions have come from the former Soviet Union. Gary Kasparov, from Azerbaijan, has been the world champion since 1985.

The female eider duck lines her nest with her own fluffy feathers. These are called eiderdown and are used for stuffing pillows and quilts.

More About...

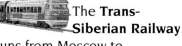

The **Trans-Siberian Railway** runs from Moscow to Vladivostok. It takes 8 days to make the journey.

The **Nenets** are reindeer herders. They live in the north of Russia, near the Arctic. They are an ancient people.

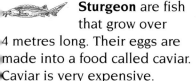

Sturgeon are fish that grow over 4 metres long. Their eggs are made into a food called caviar. Caviar is very expensive.

In the Arctic Ocean, huge **ice-breaking** ships plough through the ice. Smaller ships are then able to follow.

The Union of Soviet Socialist Republics (U.S.S.R.) no longer exists as a single country. It was made up of 15 republics, which are now independent countries. Most of these countries form the new Commonwealth of Independent States (C.I.S.). The largest new country – and the largest country in the world – is Russia. It stretches from Europe, across the Ural Mountains, to northern Asia. In the northeast it is separated from North America by the Bering Strait, a narrow strip of ocean.

The Ural Mountains run from north to south through Russia, separating the continents of Europe and Asia. The European countries have more people and industry than the Asian countries. The richest farmlands are in the southwest. Because of small harvests and poor storage and transport, there have been severe food shortages. The new countries are striving to improve this situation.

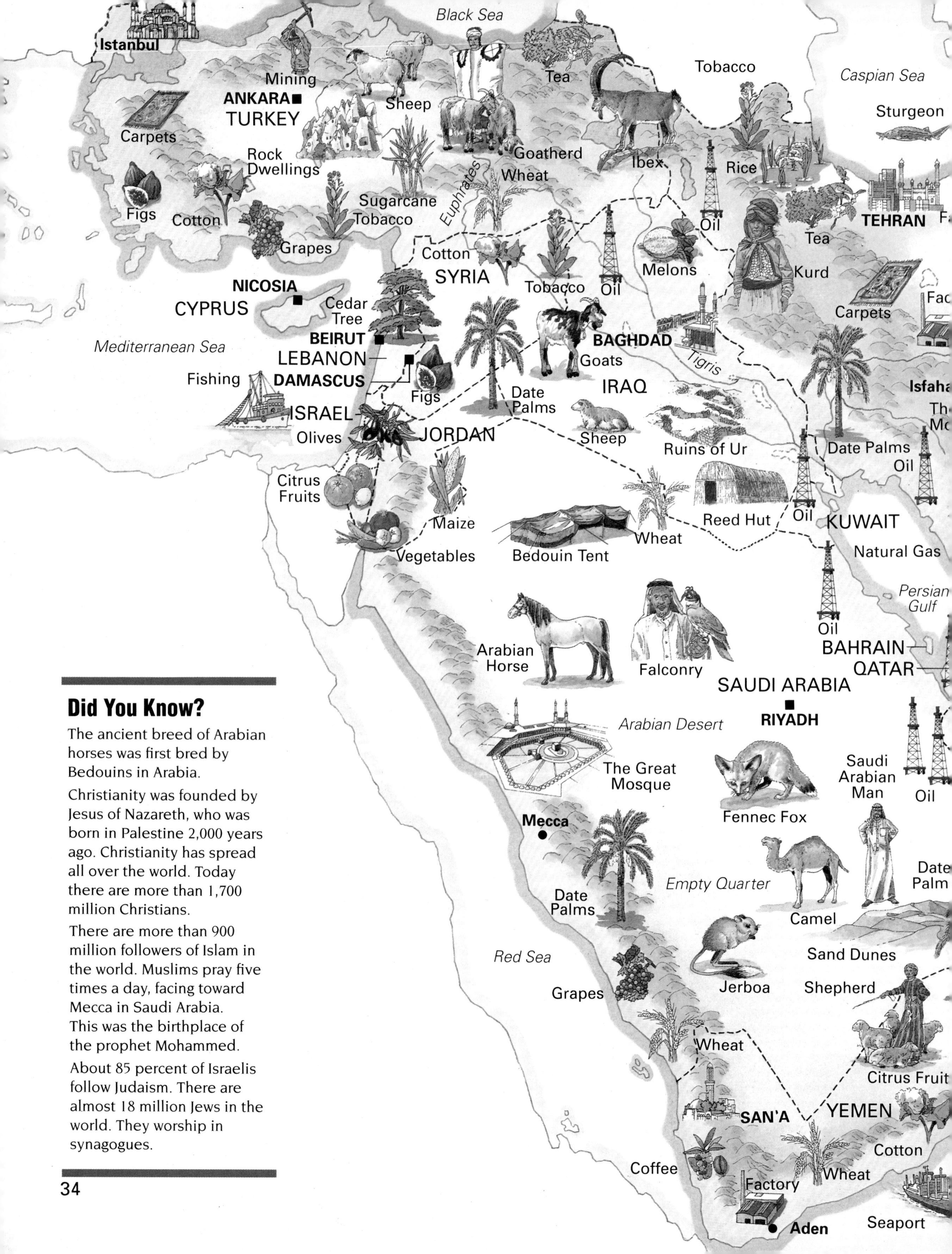
Black Sea
Istanbul
Mining
ANKARA
TURKEY
Sheep
Tea
Tobacco
Caspian Sea
Sturgeon
Carpets
Rock Dwellings
Goatherd
Ibex
Rice
Wheat
Euphrates
Sugarcane
Tobacco
Figs
Cotton
Grapes
Oil
TEHRAN
Tea
Cotton
SYRIA
Tobacco
Oil
Melons
Kurd
NICOSIA
CYPRUS
Cedar Tree
Carpets
BEIRUT
BAGHDAD
Mediterranean Sea
LEBANON
Goats
Tigris
Fishing
DAMASCUS
Figs
Date Palms
IRAQ
ISRAEL
Olives
JORDAN
Sheep
Ruins of Ur
Date Palms
Oil
Citrus Fruits
Maize
Reed Hut
Oil
KUWAIT
Wheat
Vegetables
Bedouin Tent
Natural Gas
Persian Gulf
Oil
Arabian Horse
Falconry
BAHRAIN
QATAR
SAUDI ARABIA
RIYADH
Arabian Desert
The Great Mosque
Fennec Fox
Saudi Arabian Man
Oil
Mecca
Empty Quarter
Date Palms
Camel
Red Sea
Sand Dunes
Grapes
Jerboa
Shepherd
Wheat
Citrus Fruit
SAN'A
YEMEN
Cotton
Coffee
Factory
Wheat
Aden
Seaport

Did You Know?

The ancient breed of Arabian horses was first bred by Bedouins in Arabia.

Christianity was founded by Jesus of Nazareth, who was born in Palestine 2,000 years ago. Christianity has spread all over the world. Today there are more than 1,700 million Christians.

There are more than 900 million followers of Islam in the world. Muslims pray five times a day, facing toward Mecca in Saudi Arabia. This was the birthplace of the prophet Mohammed.

About 85 percent of Israelis follow Judaism. There are almost 18 million Jews in the world. They worship in synagogues.

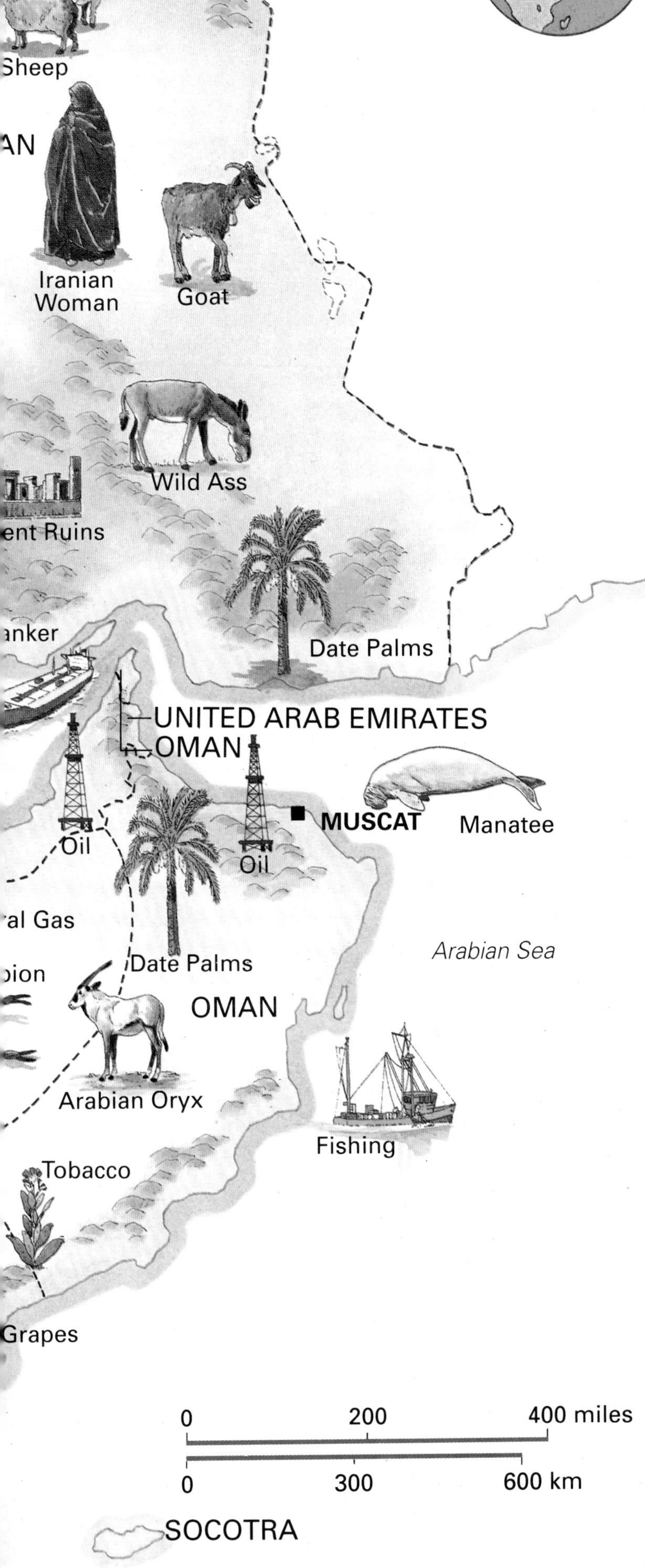

Sheep
AN
Iranian Woman
Goat
Wild Ass
ent Ruins
nker
Date Palms
UNITED ARAB EMIRATES
OMAN
Oil
Oil
MUSCAT
Manatee
al Gas
Date Palms
ion
Arabian Sea
OMAN
Arabian Oryx
Fishing
Tobacco
Grapes
0
200
400 miles
0
300
600 km
SOCOTRA

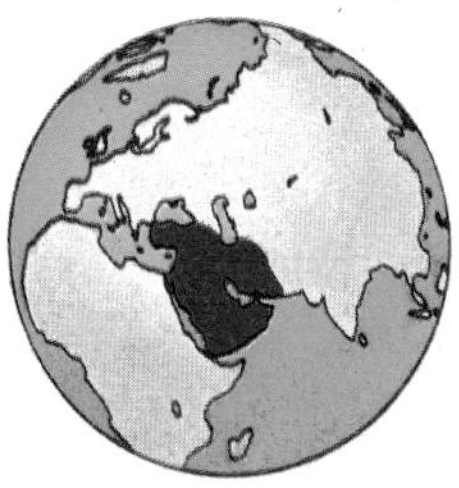

Middle East

The Middle East covers a large area of southwest Asia and northeast Africa. This region is called the 'cradle of civilization' because many ancient civilizations began here. Three world religions also started here – Christianity, Islam and Judaism. Most people in the Middle East are Muslims, followers of Islam. There are Christians and Jews, too. Most Israelis practise Judaism. The ancient Holy Land of Palestine, which is sacred to people of all three religions, is now occupied by Israel and Jordan.

The vast Arabian Desert covers parts of Saudi Arabia, Jordan, Oman, Yemen and the United Arab Emirates. The discovery of oil beneath the desert and in the Persian Gulf has made the countries around the gulf rich.

The Middle East has been marked by great unrest in recent years. Religious differences and territorial disputes remain to be solved.

More About . . .

Bedouins are tribes of Arabs who live in the Arabian Desert. Their homes are tents that they move from place to place.

Saudi Arabia has the world's largest reserves of **oil**. The oil is pumped into ships called tankers, which transport it to other countries.

Falconry is a traditional form of hunting in Saudi Arabia. Falcons are birds of prey. They hunt and eat other small animals. In captivity, they are trained to hunt other animals – but only on command.

Kurds live in the mountains where Iran, Iraq and Turkey meet. They want to form a Kurdish state where they can live by their own rules and customs.

The **ruins of Ur** are in southern Iraq. Ur was one of the most important cities of the ancient Sumerian civilization in Mesopotamia.

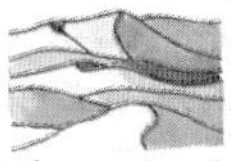

A **sand dune** is a ridge of sand formed by the wind. The wind constantly changes the shape of the dune. Part of the Arabian Desert is called the 'Empty Quarter'. It is the largest stretch of continuous sand in the world.

CHINA
TAIWAN
Pacific Ocean
HAINAN
MYANMAR
THAILAND
LAOS
VIETNAM
CAMBODIA
PHILIPPINES
BRUNEI
MALAYSIA
SARAWAK
MALAYSIA
SABAH
SINGAPORE
INDONESIA
SUMATRA
BORNEO
SULAWESI
JAVA
BALI
LOMBOK
SUMBAWA
SUMBA
FLORES
TIMOR
South China Sea
Indian Ocean
Irrawaddy
Mekong
HANOI
VIENTIANE
YANGON
BANGKOK
PHNOM PENH
Ho Chi Minh City
MANILA
KUALA LUMPUR
JAKARTA
Tea
Timber
Buddhist Monk
Temple
Working Elephant
Farmer
Timber
Peanuts
Tobacco
Bamboo
Coffee
Rice
Rice
Sugarcane
Fishing
Mining
Rice
Pelican
Jute
Temples
Mangoes
Rubber
Rice
Bananas
Beef Cattle
Fishing
Seaport
Macaque
Rice
Mining
Natural Gas
Rubber
Tobacco
Fishing
Palm Oil
Bananas
Traditional House
Rubber
Tapir
Oil
Coal
Coffee
Rice
Sugar-cane
Volcanoes
Maize
Rhinoceros
Fishing
Fishing
Tea
Komodo Dragon
Coconuts
Dayak Tribesman
Oil
Rubber
Proboscis Monkey
Orangutan
Rice
Coffee
Spices
Timber
Peppers
Coconuts
Nutmeg
Rubber
Fishing
Coconuts
Sugar-cane
Maize
Coal
Seaport
Scorpion Fish
Citrus Fruits
Mother-of-Pearl
Rice
Pineapple
Fishing
0
300
600 miles
0
400
800 km

Southeast Asia

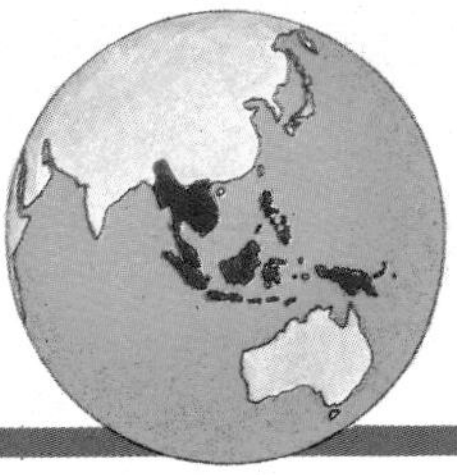

Southeast Asia is made up of more than 20,000 islands. Most of these belong to Indonesia and the Philippines. Indonesia's islands are scattered between the Asian mainland and the northern tip of Australia. Much of Southeast Asia is covered by tropical rainforest, and most of the people are farmers who live near the coast and in river valleys. Indonesia, Thailand, Vietnam and Myanmar (Burma) are among the world's top rice producers. The rainforest provides wood, such as teak and mahogany. Malaysia, Indonesia and Thailand are the world's leading rubber producers.

Many countries in the region are poor, and most cities are overcrowded. Vietnam, Laos and Cambodia have all suffered from war. In contrast, the small countries of Brunei and Singapore are both rich.

More About . . .

Most people in Myanmar are Buddhists. Between the ages of 6 and 13, boys in Myanmar spend some time as **monks**. They learn to lead a spiritual life.

Rice is the region's main crop. In many areas it is grown on terraces, which are broad steps cut into the sides of hills or mountains.

Timber, especially teak, is an important export in some Southeast Asian countries. It is used abroad for furniture and in shipbuilding.

On Java, material from the eruption of **volcanoes** produces fertile soil for growing crops.

The **Komodo dragon** is the largest lizard in the world – it can grow over 3 metres long. It lives on the Lesser Sunda Islands of Indonesia.

Rubber is made from latex, a milky gum collected from the **rubber tree**. This tree grows in many parts of Southeast Asia.

In Papua New Guinea, people believe in spirits. They build special **spirit houses** to lure any spirits away from their homes.

The city of **Singapore** is the capital of the Singapore republic. It is an international port and business centre, popular with tourists.

Oil
Palm Oil
Palm Trees
Rice
Spirit House
Palm Trees
Coconuts
PalmTrees
IRIAN JAYA
Jalé Tribesman
ONESIA
Cocoa
Puka Puka Tribesman
Coconuts
PORT MORESBY
Fishing
Bird of Paradise
PAPUA NEW GUINEA
Canoe
USTRALIA

Did You Know?

Malaysia is the world's leading producer of tin. It is also mined in Indonesia and Thailand.

Oil was discovered in Brunei in 1929. The country is ruled by a sultan. He is said to be the world's richest person.

Violent tropical storms called typhoons are common in the Philippines.

In the forests of Thailand, elephants are still used to move felled teak trees.

South Asia

To the north of India rise the snow-covered peaks of the Himalaya Mountains. The kingdoms of Bhutan and Nepal can be found there. While few people live in the mountains, it is very crowded down on the plains of India, Pakistan and Bangladesh. The Indian cities of Bombay and Calcutta also are home to millions of people. The flat central plains get very dry during the hot season. The rains, when they come, last from June to October.

In Bangladesh, most people are farmers. But the crops are often destroyed by floods. With its rapid population growth and lack of food, Bangladesh is desperately poor and dependent on foreign aid.

The Hindu and Buddhist religions started in south Asia. Today India has large numbers of Hindus, while Pakistan and Bangladesh are mainly Muslim states.

RUSSIA
Natural
AFGHANISTAN
Carpets
Pomegranates
Shepherd
Natural Gas
Wheat
Cotton
IRAN
PAKISTAN
Sheep
Rice
Arabian Sea

Did You Know?

Tigers once roamed free in India's forests. But these big cats – long hunted for their skin – are now endangered because the forests are being cut down. The tigers that remain are protected by law.

Varanasi is a holy Indian city visited by many pilgrims – Hindus, Buddhists and others. They come from all over south Asia to bathe in the River Ganges. The Hindus believe the river is sacred and will purify them.

The mongoose is a fierce little animal. It eats frogs, birds, lizards and their eggs. A mongoose throws the eggs against stones to break their shells. The Indian grey mongoose can kill a cobra.

Although Sherpas are a farming people in Nepal, they often work as guides for climbers in the Himalaya Mountains. One of these guides, Tenzing Norgay, climbed to the top of Mount Everest with the New Zealand explorer Edmund Hillary in 1953. This was the first time anyone had reached the top of the world's highest mountain.

In 1947, India gained freedom from British rule and was divided into 2 independent countries: India and Pakistan.

More About...

Making Afghan **carpets** is a traditional craft. The carpets are made from goat and sheep wool. The wool is dyed and spun. It is then woven on looms.

Polo is a sport that has been played in Pakistan for centuries. Two teams of players on horseback try to hit the ball into the goal with their mallets.

Taj Mahal means 'crown of the palace'. It was built by Emperor Shah Jahan in memory of his wife.

Mount Everest lies in the Himalaya Mountains. It stands on the border between the countries of Nepal and Tibet. At 8,845 metres, it is the world's highest mountain.

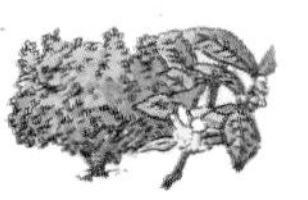

Most **tea** comes from the leaves of a small plant that is widely grown in India and Sri Lanka. The leaves are picked, dried and then sold, loose or in teabags.

Hindus believe that **cows** are sacred, so they never kill or eat them. Cows wander freely in city streets.

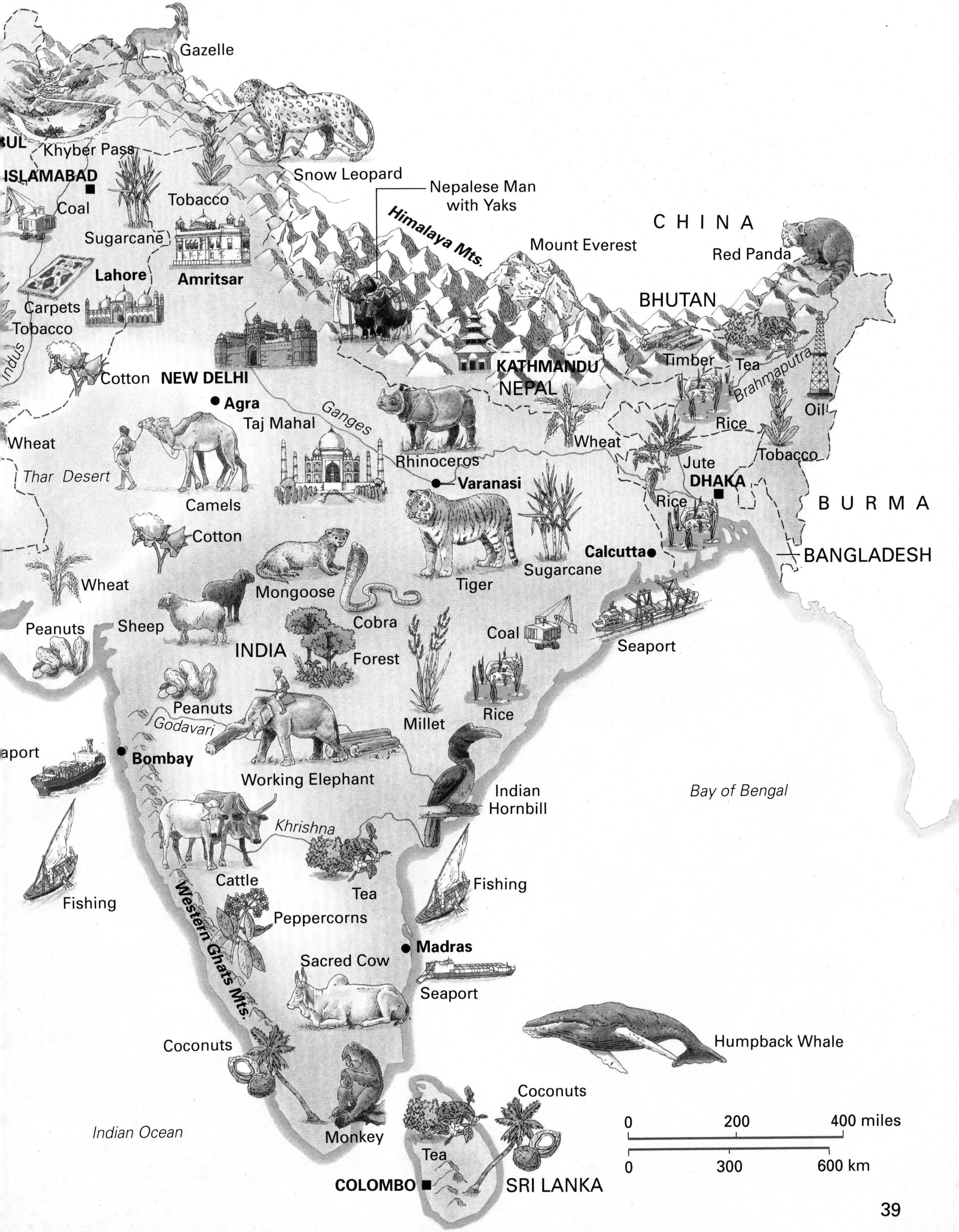
Gazelle
UL
Khyber Pass
ISLAMABAD
Coal
Tobacco
Sugarcane
Snow Leopard
Nepalese Man
with Yaks
Himalaya Mts.
CHINA
Mount Everest
Red Panda
Lahore
Amritsar
Carpets
Tobacco
BHUTAN
Indus
Cotton
NEW DELHI
Timber
Tea
KATHMANDU
NEPAL
Brahmaputra
Oil
Agra
Taj Mahal
Ganges
Wheat
Rice
Wheat
Rhinoceros
Jute
Tobacco
Thar Desert
Varanasi
DHAKA
Camels
Rice
BURMA
Cotton
Calcutta
BANGLADESH
Wheat
Mongoose
Tiger
Sugarcane
Peanuts
Sheep
Cobra
Coal
INDIA
Forest
Seaport
Peanuts
Godavari
Millet
Rice
aport
Bombay
Working Elephant
Indian
Hornbill
Bay of Bengal
Khrishna
Cattle
Tea
Fishing
Fishing
Western Ghats Mts.
Peppercorns
Madras
Sacred Cow
Seaport
Humpback Whale
Coconuts
Coconuts
0
200
400 miles
0
300
600 km
Indian Ocean
Monkey
Tea
COLOMBO
SRI LANKA

China and **Mongolia**

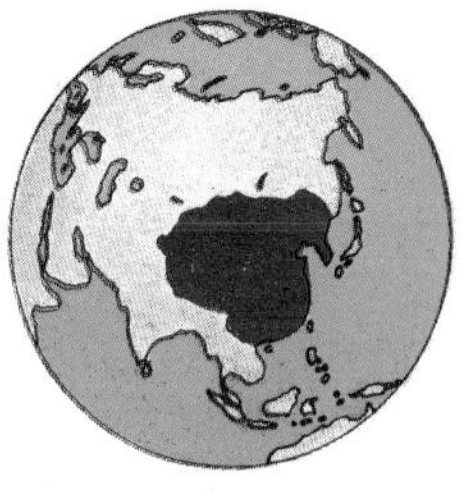

Although China is only a bit larger than the continental U.S.A. it has more than 4 times as many people. Much of China has so many mountains or is so dry that few people can live in those areas. Most people live crowded along the coast, on the plains and along China's great rivers. The soil around the Huang He – the Yellow River – is ideal for farming.

The capital of China, Beijing, is home to more than 10 million people. Shanghai, the largest city and a centre for shipping and industry, has even more people.

Off the southeast coast of mainland China is the island of Taiwan, which is a separate country. North of China is the independent country of Mongolia – and of the Gobi Desert and rolling grasslands. The Mongols are expert horsemen who follow their herds of sheep across the plains.

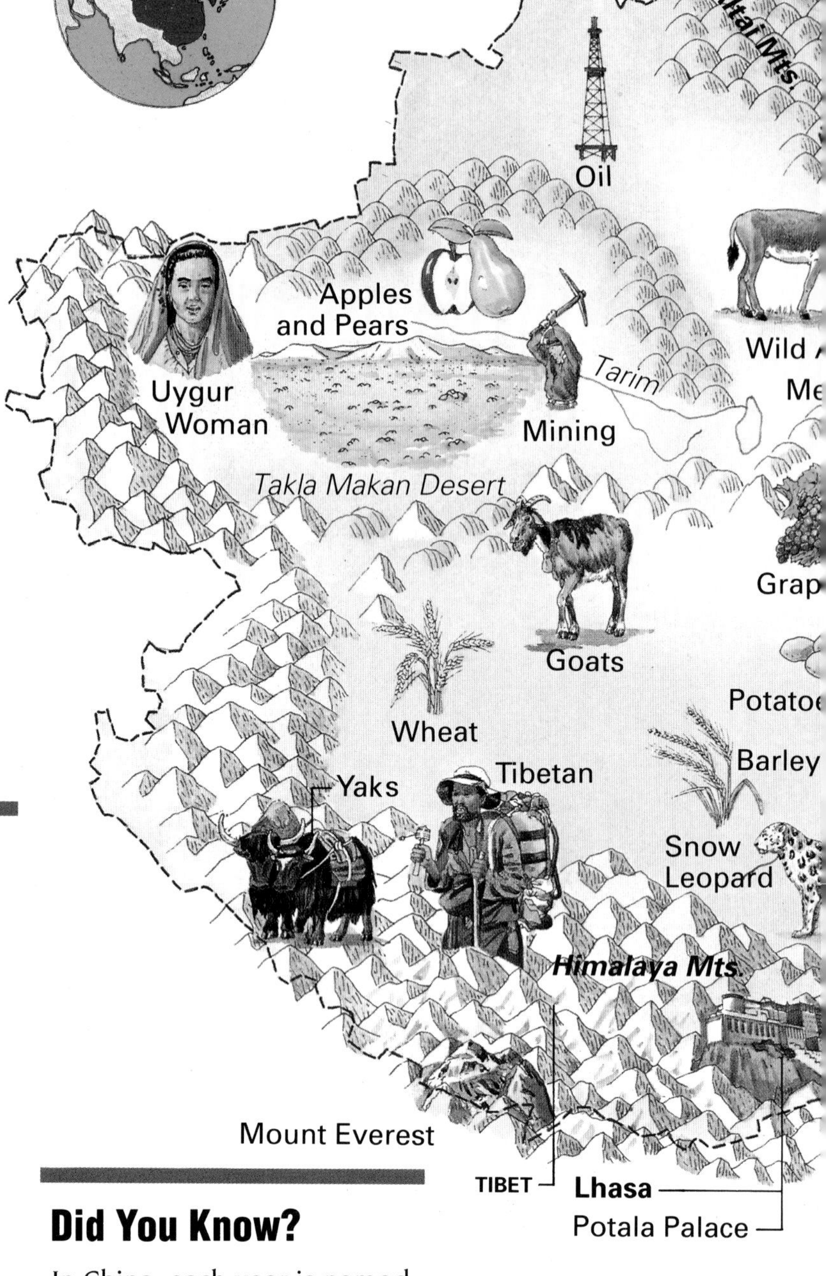
Altai Mts
Oil
Apples and Pears
Uygur Woman
Mining
Tarim
Takla Makan Desert
Goats
Wheat
Yaks
Tibetan
Barley
Snow Leopard
Himalaya Mts.
Mount Everest
TIBET
Lhasa
Potala Palace

More About . . .

The **yak** is a mountain ox that lives in the Himalayas. Yaks have long horns and shaggy hair. Tibetans use yak milk to make sour butter, which is traditionally served in tea.

The **Great Wall** of China was first built in about 214 B.C. to defend the ancient Chinese empire from its enemies in the north. It is 2,253 kilometres long and can be seen from the moon!

Bamboo is the giant of all grasses, growing as tall as some trees. Bamboo supplies food for giant pandas that live in China's bamboo forests.

Set high on a hill, the **Potala Palace** towers above the city of Lhasa in Tibet. It has 1,000 rooms. It was once the home of the Dalai Lama, Tibet's leader. Lhasa is holy to Tibetan Buddhists.

The two-humped **Bactrian camels** are found in the deserts of China and Mongolia. Their thick fur and stocky bodies help them survive the cold winters. Unfortunately, they are almost extinct in the wild.

Mongols live in round tents of felt, which they call ***gers***. They tie their gers on the backs of camels when they travel.

Did You Know?

In China, each year is named after an animal. 1995 is the year of the pig. 1996 is the year of the rat. 2000 is the year of the dragon.

There are over 130 million bicycles in China. About 30 million new bikes are made each year.

Hong Kong, with its magnificent harbour, is a leading commercial centre.

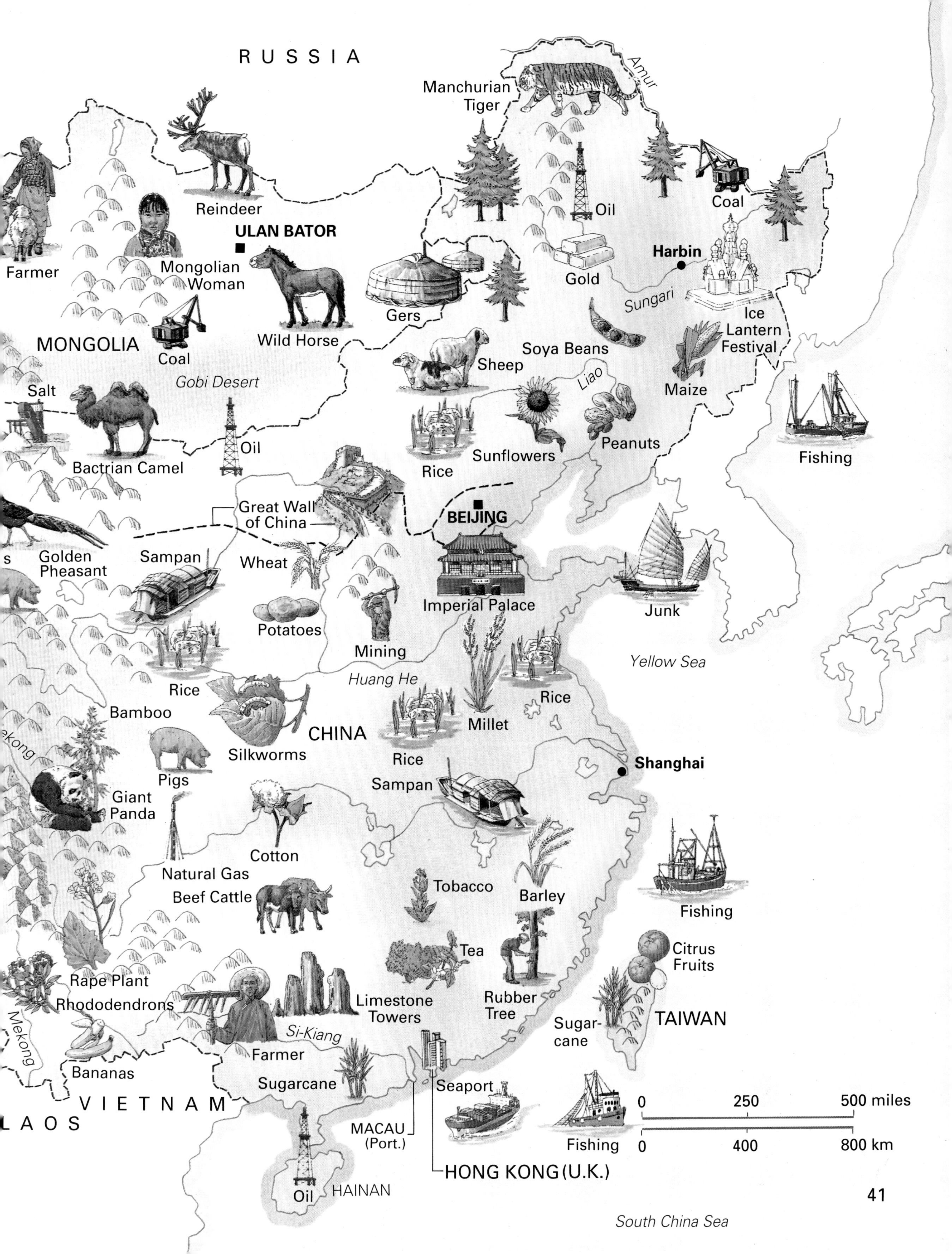
RUSSIA
Amur
Manchurian Tiger
Reindeer
ULAN BATOR
Farmer
Mongolian Woman
Oil
Coal
Harbin
Gold
Sungari
Ice Lantern Festival
Gers
Wild Horse
MONGOLIA
Coal
Sheep
Soya Beans
Maize
Gobi Desert
Liao
Salt
Oil
Peanuts
Fishing
Bactrian Camel
Sunflowers
Rice
Great Wall of China
BEIJING
Golden Pheasant
Sampan
Wheat
Imperial Palace
Junk
Potatoes
Mining
Yellow Sea
Rice
Huang He
Rice
Bamboo
Millet
CHINA
Silkworms
Rice
Shanghai
Pigs
Sampan
Giant Panda
Cotton
Natural Gas
Tobacco
Barley
Beef Cattle
Fishing
Tea
Citrus Fruits
Rape Plant
Rhododendrons
Limestone Towers
Rubber Tree
Sugar-cane
TAIWAN
Mekong
Si-Kiang
Farmer
Bananas
Sugarcane
Seaport
VIETNAM
LAOS
MACAU (Port.)
HONG KONG (U.K.)
Fishing
0 250 500 miles
0 400 800 km
Oil
HAINAN
South China Sea

Japan and Korea

Japan consists of 4 main islands: Hokkaidō, Honshū, Shikoku and Kyūshū. There are more than 3,000 smaller islands, but most of these are uninhabited. A chain of volcanic mountains runs across Japan, and there are often earthquakes. The southern Islands are hot and damp, while the northern islands are colder. Much of the land is covered with mountains and forests. Rice is the main crop. Fishing is also important. Japan is the world's leading maker of ships, cars and electronic equipment. Most Japanese enjoy a high standard of living.

Korea lies to the west of Japan. In North Korea the winters are very cold, and the climate is suitable for growing potatoes and corn. Mining and industry are important there. South Korea has a warmer climate. Most South Koreans are farmers, but the country has many factories and its products are exported all over the world.

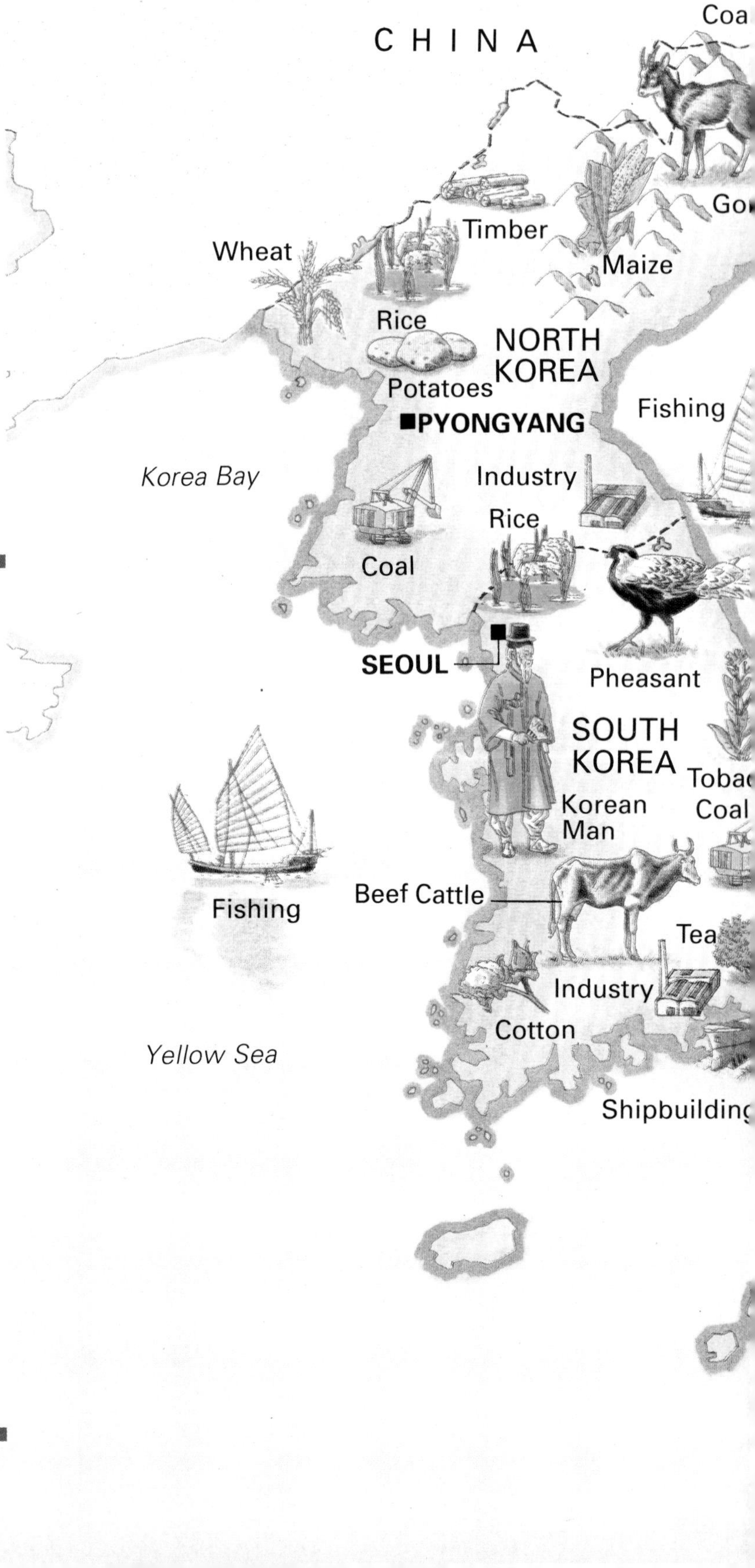

CHINA
Coa
Timber
Go
Wheat
Maize
Rice
NORTH KOREA
Potatoes
Fishing
PYONGYANG
Korea Bay
Industry
Rice
Coal
SEOUL
Pheasant
SOUTH KOREA
Toba
Coal
Korean Man
Fishing
Beef Cattle
Tea
Industry
Cotton
Yellow Sea
Shipbuildin

Did You Know?

The Japanese pay special attention to nature. In Japanese gardens, rocks, pools and waterfalls are used to create landscapes.

The cherry blossom is the national flower of Japan. Every spring people come to Ōsaka to see the cherry trees in bloom. People sit in special pavilions to enjoy the beauty of the scenery.

There are more than 100 daily newspapers in Japan, and nearly 40 million copies are sold each day. There are also 2,700 magazines.

Most of Japan's population live in towns and cities. Eleven Japanese cities have more than a million people.

In the Kinki area of Japan, fishermen use cormorants as helpers. The birds are attached to the boats by long ropes. They dive into the water after fish, but rings placed around their necks prevent them from swallowing their catch.

Mount Fuji is a volcano that towers above five beautiful lakes. It last erupted in 1707. Many Japanese believe Mount Fuji is sacred.

Visitors to a Japanese home are expected to take off their shoes and leave them at the door. Guest slippers are provided for walking in hallways, but must be removed in rooms with straw mats on the floor.

More About...

Macaques are wild monkeys that live in apan's snowy mountains. On ery cold days, the macaques eep warm by bathing in vater from hot springs.

The Shinkansen, or **bullet train**, is a modern Japanese train. It can travel at 209 kilometres per hour. Travelling nonstop, it can cover 1,175 kilometres in less than 6 hours.

The ancient art of **sumo wrestling** is the national sport of Japan. Sumo wrestlers are huge eavy men who are also very rong.

On Children's Day in Japan, many families fly **carp streamers**. These are fish-shaped streamers that are tied to bamboo poles outside their homes.

The **Ainu** were the first people to live on the islands of Japan. Today they live only on Hokkaidō island.

The famous **Torii Gate** at Miyajima rises 16 metres from the sea. It marks the entrance to a Shinto shrine.

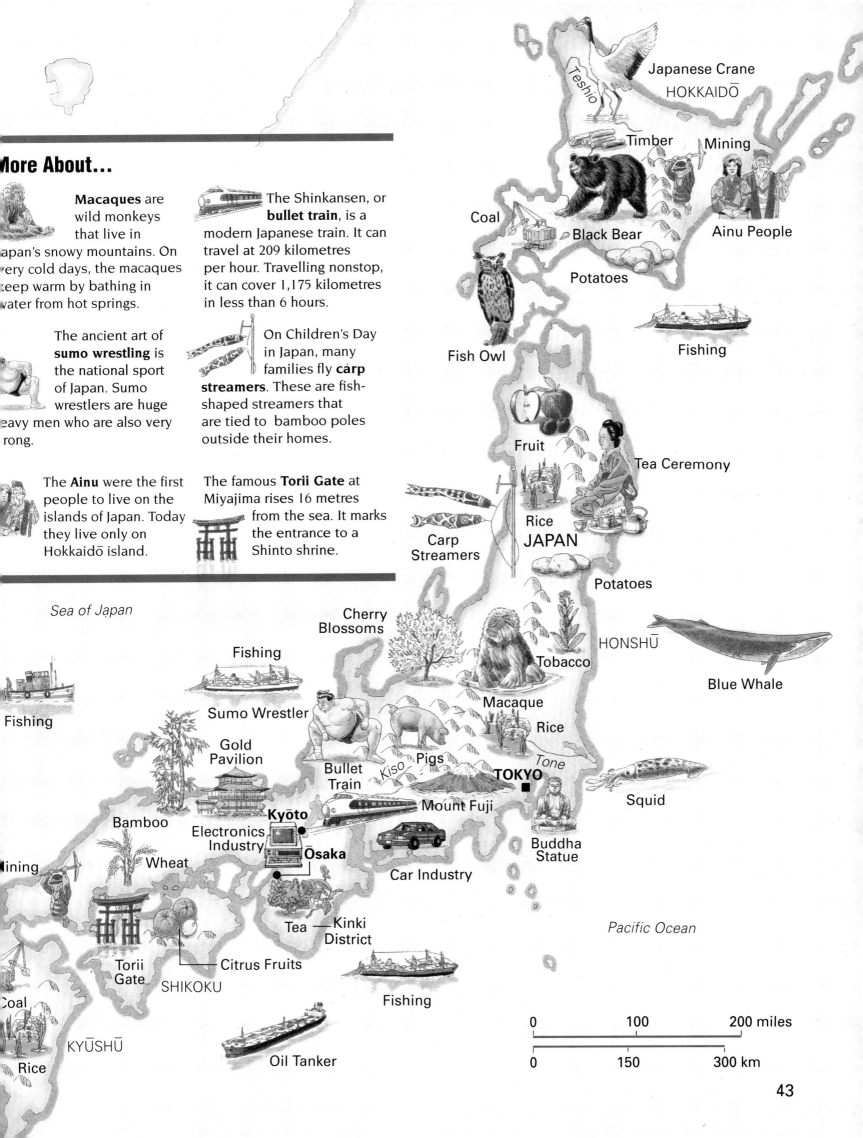

Japanese Crane
HOKKAIDŌ
Teshio
Timber
Mining
Coal
Black Bear
Ainu People
Potatoes
Fishing
Fish Owl
Fruit
Tea Ceremony
Rice
JAPAN
Carp Streamers
Potatoes

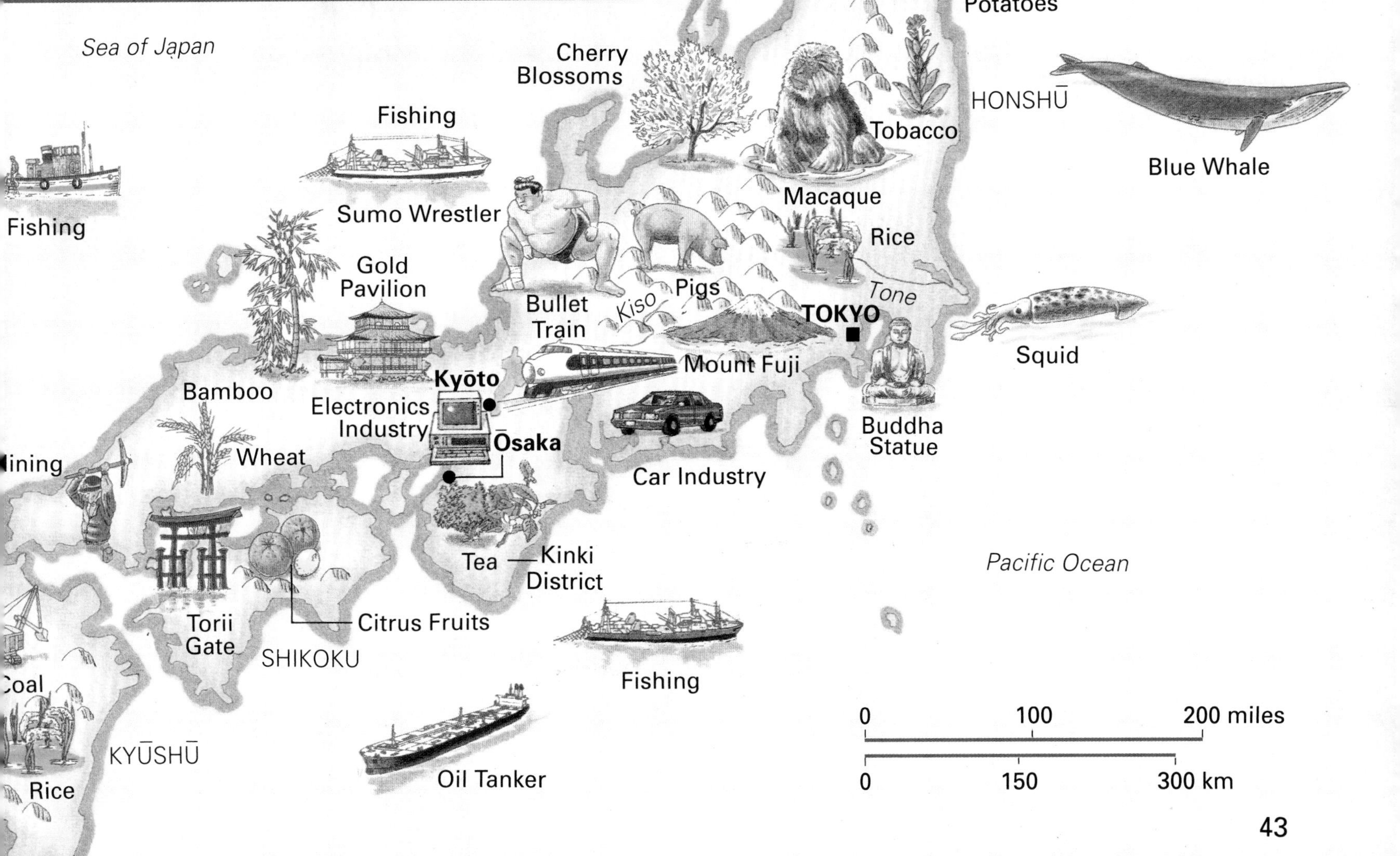
Sea of Japan
Cherry Blossoms
Fishing
HONSHŪ
Tobacco
Blue Whale
Fishing
Sumo Wrestler
Macaque
Rice
Gold Pavilion
Pigs
Tone
Bullet Train
Kiso
TOKYO
Squid
Mount Fuji
Kyōto
Bamboo
Electronics Industry
Ōsaka
Buddha Statue
ining
Wheat
Car Industry
Tea
Kinki District
Pacific Ocean
Citrus Fruits
Torii Gate
SHIKOKU
Fishing
oal
0
100
200 miles
KYŪSHŪ
Oil Tanker
0
150
300 km
Rice

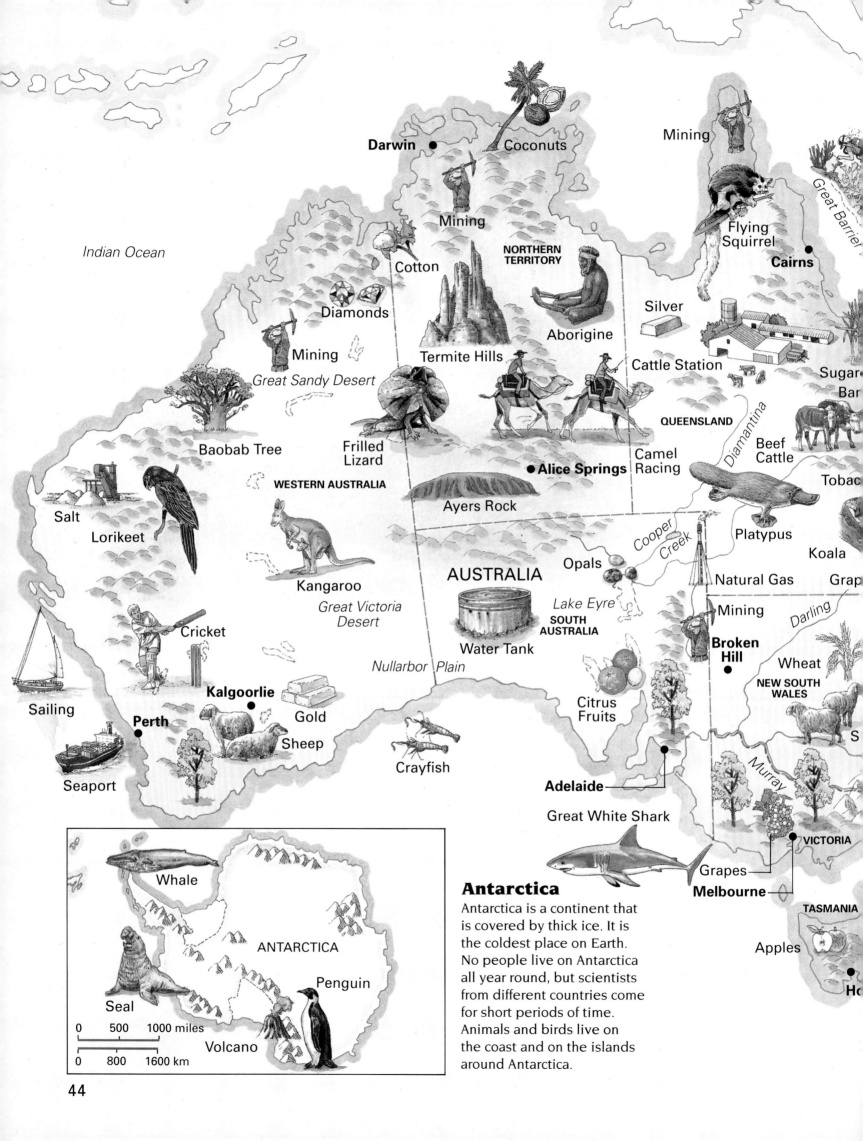

Indian Ocean
Darwin
Coconuts
Mining
Mining
NORTHERN TERRITORY
Flying Squirrel
Cairns
Cotton
Diamonds
Silver
Aborigine
Mining
Termite Hills
Cattle Station
Great Sandy Desert
QUEENSLAND
Diamantina
Beef Cattle
Baobab Tree
Frilled Lizard
Camel Racing
Alice Springs
WESTERN AUSTRALIA
Salt
Lorikeet
Ayers Rock
Platypus
Koala
Cooper Creek
Opals
Kangaroo
AUSTRALIA
Natural Gas
Great Victoria Desert
Lake Eyre
SOUTH AUSTRALIA
Mining
Darling
Cricket
Water Tank
Broken Hill
Wheat
Nullarbor Plain
NEW SOUTH WALES
Sailing
Kalgoorlie
Gold
Citrus Fruits
Perth
Sheep
Seaport
Crayfish
Murray
Adelaide
Great White Shark
VICTORIA
Grapes
Melbourne
TASMANIA
Apples

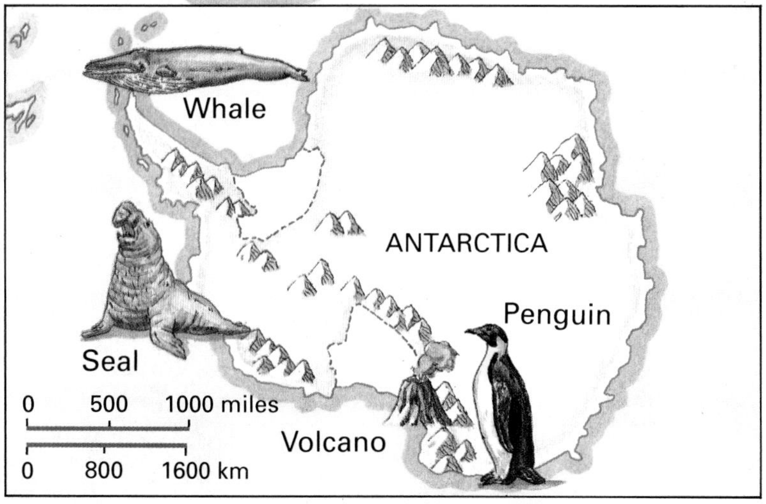

Whale
ANTARCTICA
Penguin
Seal
0 500 1000 miles
0 800 1600 km
Volcano

Antarctica

Antarctica is a continent that is covered by thick ice. It is the coldest place on Earth. No people live on Antarctica all year round, but scientists from different countries come for short periods of time. Animals and birds live on the coast and on the islands around Antarctica.

Australasia and Antarctica

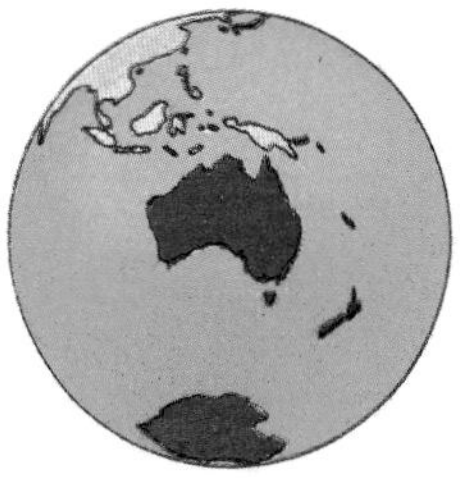

ustralia and New Zealand are
art of the region of Australasia.
Iuch of western Australia is hot
esert and few people live
ere. Many people live along
e eastern coast, where the
limate is cooler. Sydney, Australia's largest city,
on the coast. In the centre of Australia is the
utback, a dry, hot grassland where sheep are
aised. Australia is the world's principal
ool producer. Mining is important, too.
ich deposits of minerals, such as gold,
ilver, gemstones and iron are found here.

New Zealand is southeast of Australia and has a milder climate. It is divided into 2 main islands – North Island and South Island. Most New Zealanders live on North Island, where there are more large cities. South Island has good grazing land and dairy farming is important.

More About . . .

Kangaroos belong to a group of animals called marsupials. Marsupials have pouches of skin where their babies are carried after they are born.

Cricket is a sport that is as popular with Australians as it is with the British. Australian and British teams often compete.

Almost all the world's **opals** come from Australia. Opals are valued as gemstones, and they are also used in industry.

The **Great Barrier Reef** is the biggest coral reef in the world. It runs along the Queensland coast for 2,011 kilometres. The reef is very popular with divers.

The Maoris, descended from the first settlers in New Zealand, are known for their **wood carvings** – one of the traditions the Maoris are trying hard to keep alive.

The **kiwi** lives in the forests of New Zealand. This odd-looking, flightless bird uses its long bill to dig for earthworms.

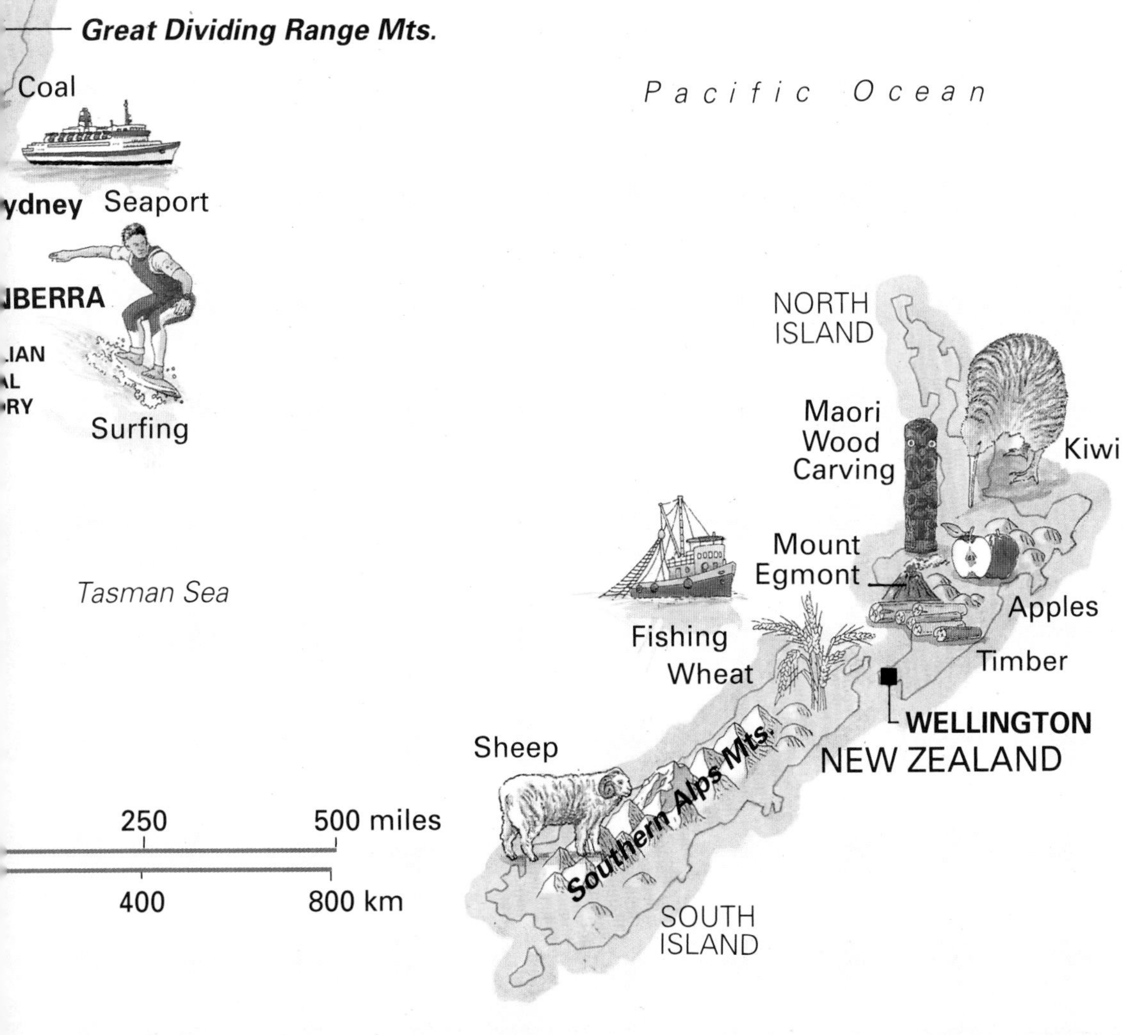

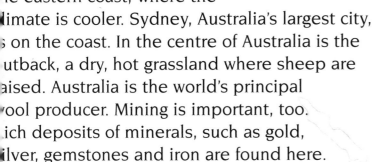

Great Dividing Range Mts.
Coal
ydney
Seaport
IBERRA
Surfing
Pacific Ocean
Tasman Sea
NORTH ISLAND
Maori Wood Carving
Kiwi
Mount Egmont
Apples
Fishing
Wheat
Timber
WELLINGTON
NEW ZEALAND
Sheep
Southern Alps Mts.
SOUTH ISLAND
250
500 miles
400
800 km

Did You Know?

Before Europeans arrived in 1770, the aborigines were the only people in Australia. Aborigines roamed the continent, hunting and gathering food, for at least 30,000 years. The land is still sacred to them, and their legend about its creation is called Dreamtime.

The baobab is a type of bottle tree. Its swollen trunk stores water to help it live through the dry season.

Ayers Rock rises 348 metres above the central Australian desert. To the aborigines, this vast red rock is a sacred place called Uluru. At the rock's base are caves, which have paintings on the walls.

Map Index